Java JUMBLE®

Henri Arnold,
Bob Lee,
and
Mike Argirion

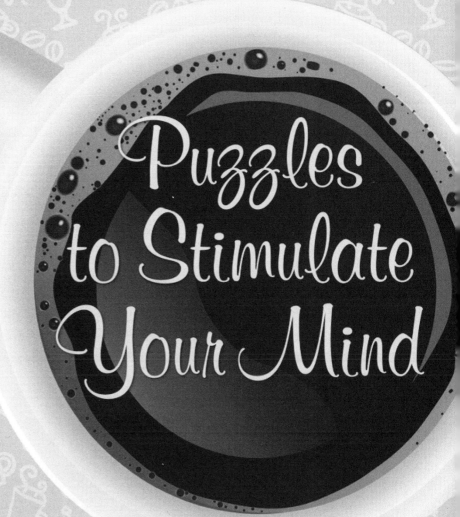

*Puzzles
to Stimulate
Your Mind*

TRIUMPH
BOOKS

This book is available in quantity at special discounts
for your group or organization.

For further information, contact:

Triumph Books
542 South Dearborn Street
Suite 750
Chicago, Illinois 60605
(312) 939-3330
Fax (312) 663-3557
www.triumphbooks.com

Printed in U.S.A.

ISBN: 978-1-60078-415-6

Design by Sue Knopf

Contents

Classic Puzzles
1–25...Page 1

Daily Puzzles
26–160...Page 27

Challenger Puzzles
161–180...Page 163

Answers
Page 184

Java JUMBLE®

Classic Puzzles

JUMBLE®

Unscramble these four Jumbles, one letter to each square, to form four ordinary words.

MASCH
C H A S M

DYNAH
H A N D Y

MAIRDY
◯ ◯ ◯ ◯ ◯

NIFTIE
◯ ◯ ◯ ◯ ◯

WHEN SHE GOT MARRIED, SHE WENT FROM---

Now arrange the circled letters to form the surprise answer, as suggested by the above cartoon.

Print answer here ◯◯◯◯◯◯ TO ◯◯◯◯

Unscramble these four Jumbles, one letter to each square, to form four ordinary words.

PALLE

CHEEN

THAAMS

PECDIT

I'll hide back there

WHAT THE FARMER DID TO STYMIE THE CHICKEN THIEF.

Now arrange the circled letters to form the surprise answer, as suggested by the above cartoon.

Print " ⃝⃝⃝⃝⃝⃝⃝ " A ⃝⃝⃝⃝⃝
answer
here

JUMBLE®

Unscramble these four Jumbles, one letter to each square, to form four ordinary words.

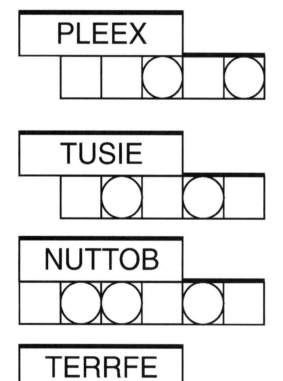

PLEEX

TUSIE

NUTTOB

TERRFE

But, Miss Spindlehoff, I told you I'd pay you next week

I've heard that before

WHEN HE RECEIVED THE EVICTION NOTICE, HE---

Now arrange the circled letters to form the surprise answer, as suggested by the above cartoon.

Print answer here

 "  "

JUMBLE®

Unscramble these four Jumbles, one letter to
each square, to form four ordinary words.

BISCA

REGUP

TROICE

RAWHEL

It's my
turn to
go up

No, it's
my turn

They need
separate
missions

WHAT THE FEUDING
ASTRONAUTS
NEEDED.

Now arrange the circled letters to form the
surprise answer, as suggested by the above
cartoon.

*Print
answer
here*   " "

JUMBLE®

Unscramble these four Jumbles, one letter to each square, to form four ordinary words.

EGGOU

HYSUB

PAMERC

PEWDOL

THE SHOEMAKER'S SOLE COMPANION...

Now arrange the circled letters to form the surprise answer, as suggested by the above cartoon.

Print answer here ○○○ A ○○○○○

Unscramble these four Jumbles, one letter to
each square, to form four ordinary words.

LUTOC

THABI

LABDAL

JELIAD

This is
hard to
believe

Of course,
it's fiction

EDITOR

WHAT HE ENDED
UP WITH WHEN
HE FINISHED HIS
SHORT STORY.

Now arrange the circled letters to form the
surprise answer, as suggested by the above
cartoon.

Print answer here A "◯◯◯◯◯" ◯◯◯◯◯

JUMBLE®

Unscramble these four Jumbles, one letter to
each square, to form four ordinary words.

DEROO

CUNOE

GORUME

GNOBLE

Let's see your IDs.
You guys behave

Don't
mess with
him

BAR

THE BASKETBALL
PLAYER WORKED
AT THE COLLEGE
BAR BECAUSE HE
WAS A----

Now arrange the circled letters to form the
surprise answer, as suggested by the above
cartoon.

**Print
answer
here**

" "

JUMBLE.

Unscramble these four Jumbles, one letter to each square, to form four ordinary words.

CNARF

YILIC

LIFFUT

GAZZIG

Hi, Uncle Ted

How's school? Making grades? Any girlfriends?

WHAT THE DETEC-TIVE WAS GOOD AT DOING AT A FAMILY GATHERING.

Now arrange the circled letters to form the surprise answer, as suggested by the above cartoon.

Print answer here " _____ "

JUMBLE®

Unscramble these four Jumbles, one letter to
each square, to form four ordinary words.

VELOR

ASTEE

CHYPIS

DRAUWP

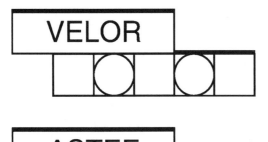

Hey, Ralph,
I hear
you're
leaving

I'm picking up
towels all day

HE QUIT HIS JOB
AT THE SAUNA
BECAUSE IT WAS
A REAL---

Now arrange the circled letters to form the
surprise answer, as suggested by the above
cartoon.

*Print answer
here* " ⭘⭘⭘⭘⭘ " ⭘⭘⭘⭘

JUMBLE®

Unscramble these four Jumbles, one letter to each square, to form four ordinary words.

CIHRB

LIBOR

DEWPOR

FLEMUF

24!
The next
one is 30!

Wait your turn, Bobby

12+12 =
15 +15 =

WHAT THE
MATH TEACHER
CONSIDERED THE
PRECOCIOUS PUPIL.

Now arrange the circled letters to form the surprise answer, as suggested by the above cartoon.

**Print
answer A
here** " ⃝⃝⃝⃝⃝⃝⃝⃝ " ⃝⃝⃝⃝⃝

JUMBLE®

Unscramble these four Jumbles, one letter to
each square, to form four ordinary words.

CLIVI

GATEA

STIMCY

RUHNGY

You're looking fit, Jim

No starches,
no fat. I
lost 15 pounds

"GIRTH" CAN BE
TURNED INTO
THIS.

Now arrange the circled letters to form the
surprise answer, as suggested by the above
cartoon.

Print answer here " ◯◯◯◯◯ "

JUMBLE®

Unscramble these four Jumbles, one letter to each square, to form four ordinary words.

ZYIZD

SIRUV

AVGASE

HATTUG

Sally, is that you?

WHAT SHE WORE TO THE COSTUME PARTY.

Now arrange the circled letters to form the surprise answer, as suggested by the above cartoon.

Print answer here A ◯◯◯'◯ ◯◯◯◯◯

JUMBLE®

Unscramble these four Jumbles, one letter to each square, to form four ordinary words.

STRON

GYTAN

CODEED

HARMIO

I had a good feeling about this

Aah, you were just lucky

WHEN HE WON THE POKER TOURNAMENT, HE KNEW IT WAS----

Now arrange the circled letters to form the surprise answer, as suggested by the above cartoon.

Print answer here

JUMBLE®

Unscramble these four Jumbles, one letter to each square, to form four ordinary words.

MURYM

CIKHT

PATELA

TAIROD

Did you hear about Lucille and Fred?

WHAT SHE GOT WHEN SHE WORKED IN HER GARDEN.

Now arrange the circled letters to form the surprise answer, as suggested by the above cartoon.

Print answer here ◯◯◯ " ◯◯◯◯ "

JUMBLE®

Unscramble these four Jumbles, one letter to each square, to form four ordinary words.

RUPPE

ELCEX

CRASAF

NITIVE

Whatever you say, sir

He's a born leader

EASY FOR A GENERAL TO COMMAND.

Now arrange the circled letters to form the surprise answer, as suggested by the above cartoon.

Print answer here

JUMBLE®

Unscramble these four Jumbles, one letter to each square, to form four ordinary words.

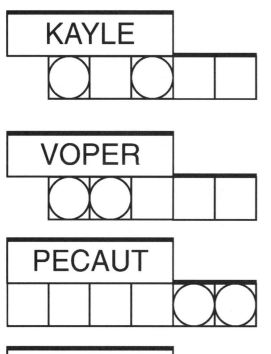

KAYLE

VOPER

PECAUT

STIVEN

Another A. Well done, Richard

WHEN HE TOOK THE ASTRONOMY CLASS, HE BECAME A----

Now arrange the circled letters to form the surprise answer, as suggested by the above cartoon.

Print answer here "◯◯◯◯◯" ◯◯◯◯◯

JUMBLE®

Unscramble these four Jumbles, one letter to each square, to form four ordinary words.

PERPI

NYKAL

PHYSEC

PARTTE

He's a classically trained pianist

With a good ear

WHAT IT TAKES TO WRITE A SONG.

Now arrange the circled letters to form the surprise answer, as suggested by the above cartoon.

Print answer here

☐☐☐☐☐☐ **AND** ☐☐☐☐☐☐☐

JUMBLE®

Unscramble these four Jumbles, one letter to each square, to form four ordinary words.

NOUGY

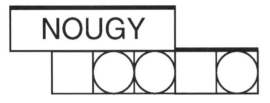

HERBT

CHANIG

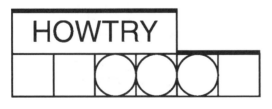

HOWTRY

It had to be somebody else

Isn't this your ball?

WHEN JUNIOR SAID HE DIDN'T BREAK THE WINDOW, DAD SAW---

Now arrange the circled letters to form the surprise answer, as suggested by the above cartoon.

Print answer here

  IT

Unscramble these four Jumbles, one letter to each square, to form four ordinary words.

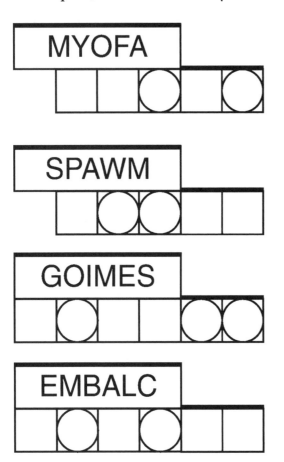

MYOFA

SPAWM

GOIMES

EMBALC

We'll need a tall guy

WHAT THE PRISON BASKETBALL TEAM SADLY LACKED.

Now arrange the circled letters to form the surprise answer, as suggested by the above cartoon.

Print answer here " ◯◯◯◯ " ◯◯◯◯◯◯

JUMBLE®

Unscramble these four Jumbles, one letter to each square, to form four ordinary words.

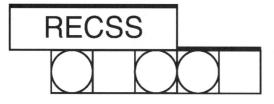

RECSS

PHLYS

SLAPOT

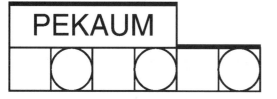

PEKAUM

Think these will wow the girls?

IMPORTANT WHEN SHOPPING FOR EYEGLASSES.

Now arrange the circled letters to form the surprise answer, as suggested by the above cartoon.

Print answer here

JUMBLE®

Unscramble these four Jumbles, one letter to each square, to form four ordinary words.

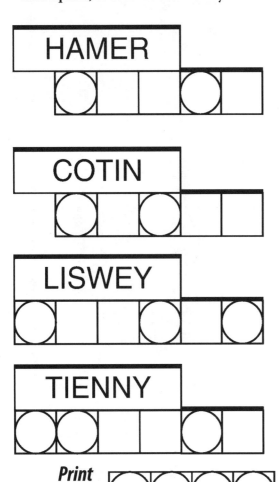

HAMER

COTIN

LISWEY

TIENNY

Now remember, Hortense is married to Horace and Sally is...

HOW THE SOCIAL CLIMBERS AVOIDED BEING OUTSIDERS.

Now arrange the circled letters to form the surprise answer, as suggested by the above cartoon.

Print answer here

JUMBLE®

Unscramble these four Jumbles, one letter to each square, to form four ordinary words.

URFOL

SWEYN

OBNIBB

DRENGE

...and don't come back

Lobby, please

WHAT HE EXPERI-ENCED WHEN HE LOST THE ACCOUNT.

Now arrange the circled letters to form the surprise answer, as suggested by the above cartoon.

Print answer here A "⬡⬡⬡⬡⬡⬡"

JUMBLE®

Unscramble these four Jumbles, one letter to
each square, to form four ordinary words.

BELLI

LOFOR

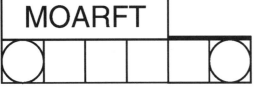

HEMMAY

MOARFT

Joe, you look
like a thug

WHEN THE
PATROLMAN WENT
UNDERCOVER,
HE WAS---

Now arrange the circled letters to form the
surprise answer, as suggested by the above
cartoon.

Print answer here  " "

JUMBLE®

Unscramble these four Jumbles, one letter to each square, to form four ordinary words.

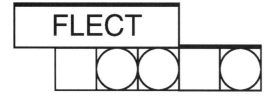

FLECT

RABOX

EVITLY

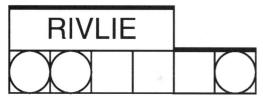

RIVLIE

Good news! My parents are coming for two weeks

It'll be like the big bang

WHICH OF EINSTEIN'S THEORIES CAN APPLY TO MARRIAGE?

Now arrange the circled letters to form the surprise answer, as suggested by the above cartoon.

Print answer here "◯◯◯◯◯◯◯◯-◯◯◯"

JUMBLE®

Unscramble these four Jumbles, one letter to
each square, to form four ordinary words.

TIFFY

PIMSK

REGAHN

WEVILS

Sure beats working
midnight to eight

EVEN A MORNING
DAY-CARE WORKER
CAN END UP
HERE.

Now arrange the circled letters to form the
surprise answer, as suggested by the above
cartoon.

Print
answer THE "⬤⬤⬤⬤⬤" ⬤⬤⬤⬤⬤
here

Java JUMBLE®

Daily Puzzles

JUMBLE®

Unscramble these four Jumbles, one letter to each square, to form four ordinary words.

MESOO

SHAQU

CECHIT

LANDAV

Steady as a rock

His dexterity is remarkable

WHEN THE CUS-
TOMERS OBSERVED
THE WATCHMAKER,
THEY MARVELED
AT THE—

Now arrange the circled letters to form the surprise answer, as suggested by the above cartoon.

Print answer here " ◯◯◯◯◯ " OF ◯◯◯◯

JUMBLE®

Unscramble these four Jumbles, one letter to each square, to form four ordinary words.

STUJO

URROF

TETINY

NATFUL

Saw, please

WHAT IT TOOK TO REPAIR THE ATHLETE'S KNEE.

Now arrange the circled letters to form the surprise answer, as suggested by the above cartoon.

Print answer here

A " ⬡⬡⬡⬡⬡ " ⬡⬡⬡⬡⬡⬡

JUMBLE®

Unscramble these four Jumbles, one letter to
each square, to form four ordinary words.

FECAH
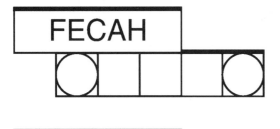

ELUSO
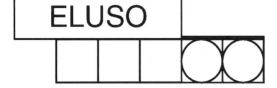

TRAROM

MORLAN

Two more runs

The ballgame
helps him
concentrate

WHY THE MAESTRO
LISTENED TO THE
BALLGAME.

Now arrange the circled letters to form the
surprise answer, as suggested by the above
cartoon.

Print
answer TO ⬡⬡⬡⬡⬡ THE " ⬡⬡⬡⬡⬡ "
here

JUMBLE®

Unscramble these four Jumbles, one letter to
each square, to form four ordinary words.

ORRGI

SHYKU

WARMOR

TEGOTH

This beats
driving

N.Y. to L.A.
in five hours

PREFERRED WHEN
TRAVELING CROSS-
COUNTRY.

Now arrange the circled letters to form the
surprise answer, as suggested by the above
cartoon.

Print answer here THE " ◯◯◯◯◯ " ◯◯◯

JUMBLE®

Unscramble these four Jumbles, one letter to
each square, to form four ordinary words.

DACKE

DUCIL

RANLEY

AIBBED

Lights out, boys

Time to get
some sleep

See you
tomorrow,
Ralph

WHAT THE PATRONS
DID WHEN THE
BAR CLOSED AT
MIDNIGHT.

Now arrange the circled letters to form the
surprise answer, as suggested by the above
cartoon.

*Print
answer
here*

IT A "◯◯◯"

32

JUMBLE®

Unscramble these four Jumbles, one letter to each square, to form four ordinary words.

RIVOY

YEMON

DEFILD

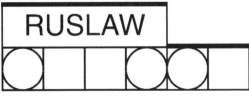

RUSLAW

I get the top bunk

Whatever you say

WHERE HE ENDED UP WHEN HE GOT ARRESTED.

Now arrange the circled letters to form the surprise answer, as suggested by the above cartoon.

Print answer IN THE " ⬭⬭⬭⬭⬭⬭⬭⬭⬭⬭⬭ " *here*

33

JUMBLE

Unscramble these four Jumbles, one letter to
each square, to form four ordinary words.

VEELA

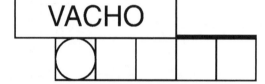

VACHO

NEURED

LADRIA

His leg's better. Now
he won't leave my side

WHEN SHE TOOK
CARE OF THE
INJURED PUPPY,
HE---

Now arrange the circled letters to form the
surprise answer, as suggested by the above
cartoon.

Print answer here "  "

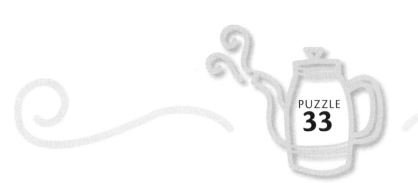

JUMBLE®

Unscramble these four Jumbles, one letter to
each square, to form four ordinary words.

KINDE

USCOT

LAMORF

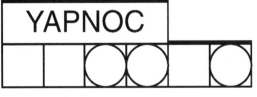

YAPNOC

WHAT SHE FACED
WHEN HE TRIED
TO CUT IN.

Now arrange the circled letters to form the
surprise answer, as suggested by the above
cartoon.

*Print
answer
here*

Unscramble these four Jumbles, one letter to
each square, to form four ordinary words.

HEMIC

GEALE

FRIEVY

SPYDOR

I'm on call
24 hours
a day

Your hours
are worse
than mine

WHAT THE OBSTE-
TRICIAN AND
TRUCK DRIVER
DISCUSSED.

Now arrange the circled letters to form the
surprise answer, as suggested by the above
cartoon.

*Print answer
here*

36

JUMBLE

Unscramble these four Jumbles, one letter to each square, to form four ordinary words.

MOECT

ANUFA

DETHOB

HANCUL

This is a popular color and very durable

Stan has turned into an expert

WHEN HE BOUGHT THE FABRIC STORE, HE BECAME A---

Now arrange the circled letters to form the surprise answer, as suggested by the above cartoon.

Print answer here ◯◯◯ OF THE " ◯◯◯◯◯ "

JUMBLE®

Unscramble these four Jumbles, one letter to
each square, to form four ordinary words.

ARGIN

SUAPE

DELOON

BRUHEC

Harold, are we engaged
or not?

We'll talk
about it —

SOUNDED LIKE
THIS TO HIS
GIRLFRIEND.

Now arrange the circled letters to form the
surprise answer, as suggested by the above
cartoon.

Print answer here THE ◯◯◯◯◯◯◯◯◯

JUMBLE®

Unscramble these four Jumbles, one letter to each square, to form four ordinary words.

WHYSO

LESOO

SNORPI

INGARD

Psst! Wanna buy a watch? How 'bout a ring?

No thank you. Have a nice day

EASY TO AVOID WITH A SUNNY DISPOSITION.

Now arrange the circled letters to form the surprise answer, as suggested by the above cartoon.

Print answer A here

" ◯◯◯◯◯ " ◯◯◯◯◯◯◯

JUMBLE®

Unscramble these four Jumbles, one letter to each square, to form four ordinary words.

YULST

VURCE

SORABB

AFDACE

Maybe we should go in

Just a sprinkle. Full speed ahead

WHAT THE GOLFING ADMIRAL DID WHEN IT BEGAN RAINING.

Now arrange the circled letters to form the surprise answer, as suggested by the above cartoon.

Print answer here ◯◯◯◯◯ **THE** ◯◯◯◯◯◯

JUMBLE®

Unscramble these four Jumbles, one letter to
each square, to form four ordinary words.

CASHO

INFEK

DUBACT

TIGRUD

I can't remember
all those dates

I hope you
remember
ours tonight

F

WHY THE STUDENT
DROPPED THE
HISTORY CLASS.

Now arrange the circled letters to form the
surprise answer, as suggested by the above
cartoon.

**Print
answer
here** IT ⬜⬜⬜ ⬜⬜ " ⬜⬜⬜⬜⬜⬜ "

JUMBLE®

Unscramble these four Jumbles, one letter to
each square, to form four ordinary words.

NUIFY

LHEVO

SACCUT

HUPNAC

You won't lose
weight that way

It's my
own special
plan

WHAT HIS WIFE
CONCLUDED HE
HAD WHEN HE
WENT ON AN
ICE-CREAM DIET.

Now arrange the circled letters to form the
surprise answer, as suggested by the above
cartoon.

Print answer **A** *here* " ⬡⬡⬡ " ⬡⬡⬡⬡⬡⬡⬡

JUMBLE®

Unscramble these four Jumbles, one letter to each square, to form four ordinary words.

TUILB

PHACT

STUMEK

LEEXUD

The brass section is off. Start again

He's a stern taskmaster

WHY THE ORCHES-TRA FUNCTIONED LIKE CLOCKWORK.

Now arrange the circled letters to form the surprise answer, as suggested by the above cartoon.

Print answer here IT ◯◯◯◯ " ◯◯◯◯ "

JUMBLE®

Unscramble these four Jumbles, one letter to each square, to form four ordinary words.

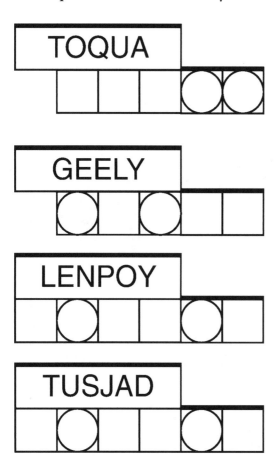

TOQUA

GEELY

LENPOY

TUSJAD

Psst—did you hear about Sen. Snort?

PRESS

OFTEN NEEDED FOR A COLUMN.

Now arrange the circled letters to form the surprise answer, as suggested by the above cartoon.

Print answer here **A**

44

Unscramble these four Jumbles, one letter to
each square, to form four ordinary words.

DESOU

COITS

GININN

VIRFED

We'll need another
10,000 recruits

...and build
more barracks

IN THE MILITARY,
ADDITIONS CAN'
CREATE----

Now arrange the circled letters to form the
surprise answer, as suggested by the above
cartoon.

Print answer here

JUMBLE®

Unscramble these four Jumbles, one letter to each square, to form four ordinary words.

GYTIN

T I N G Y

EDGUF

F U D G E

GOOLIG

G I G O L O

DEMUGS

S M U D G E

Don't touch

He's a neat freak

THE FINGERPRINT EXPERT HAD A CLEAN DESK BECAUSE HE WAS----

Now arrange the circled letters to form the surprise answer, as suggested by the above cartoon.

Print answer here

G O O D AT " D U S T I N G "

46

JUMBLE®

Unscramble these four Jumbles, one letter to
each square, to form four ordinary words.

USSOE

ONIGG

FRUIPY

NAEVLE

SCREECH

She's
awful

Sounds like a
sick owl

WHAT AN "ORGAN"
CAN PRODUCE.

Now arrange the circled letters to form the
surprise answer, as suggested by the above
cartoon.

Print answer here A " ◯◯◯◯◯ "

JUMBLE®

Unscramble these four Jumbles, one letter to each square, to form four ordinary words.

GRAWE

MIRGE

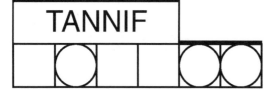

TANNIF

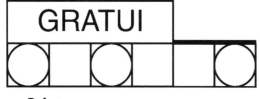

GRATUI

It's pouring

BONG BONG

That's our weather warning system

WHEN THE STORM HIT, THE CHURCH BELLS IN THE SMALL TOWN WERE——

Now arrange the circled letters to form the surprise answer, as suggested by the above cartoon.

Print answer here " ⃝⃝⃝⃝⃝⃝⃝ " ⃝⃝⃝

JUMBLE®

Unscramble these four Jumbles, one letter to each square, to form four ordinary words.

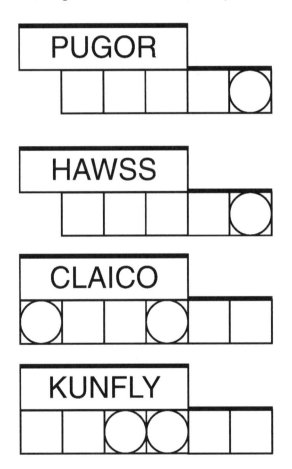

PUGOR

HAWSS

CLAICO

KUNFLY

Your smile is still the same

WHAT THE AGING BEAUTY WAS ABLE TO KEEP WHEN SHE HAD A FACE-LIFT.

Now arrange the circled letters to form the surprise answer, as suggested by the above cartoon.

Print answer here HER

JUMBLE®

Unscramble these four Jumbles, one letter to
each square, to form four ordinary words.

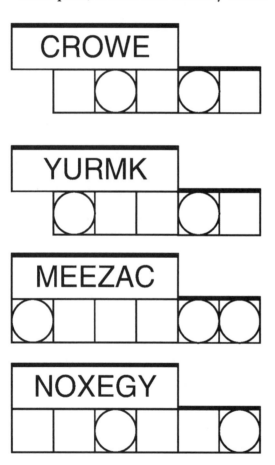

CROWE

YURMK

MEEZAC

NOXEGY

This job
gives me
security
and benefits

WHY HE WORKED
AT THE MINT.

Now arrange the circled letters to form the
surprise answer, as suggested by the above
cartoon.

*Print answer
here* TO

JUMBLE®

Unscramble these four Jumbles, one letter to each square, to form four ordinary words.

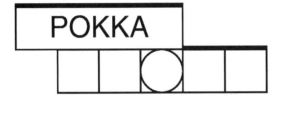

POKKA

HIDUM

MUTTUL

GOOSTE

Why, I never...!

GO
TEAM!

We need
another
round

FREE COCKTAILS
ON A FLIGHT CAN
CAUSE SOME PAS-
SENGERS TO BE----

Now arrange the circled letters to form the
surprise answer, as suggested by the above
cartoon.

Print answer here  , "  "

JUMBLE®

Unscramble these four Jumbles, one letter to
each square, to form four ordinary words.

MIDIO

LENEK

BUHSIL

ZIFLEZ

Don't stuff yourself with all that food
on the cruise, Charlie

WHAT THE ASSIS-
TANT DID WHEN
THE TAXIDERMIST
TOOK A VACATION.

Now arrange the circled letters to form the
surprise answer, as suggested by the above
cartoon.

Print answer here " ◯◯◯◯◯◯ " ◯◯

JUMBLE®

Unscramble these four Jumbles, one letter to
each square, to form four ordinary words.

KOWEA

LYRDY

HENUCQ

DRAILZ

All done

That
was
fast

ARRESTED

THE OUTLAWS
RESPECTED THE
ARTIST BECAUSE
HE WAS——

Now arrange the circled letters to form the
surprise answer, as suggested by the above
cartoon.

**Print
answer
here**
ON THE " "

JUMBLE®

Unscramble these four Jumbles, one letter to each square, to form four ordinary words.

TAPAD

RUYLB

VOXCEN

EDGERD

That really shows off your shape and it's on sale

I went from a 12 to an 8

WHAT KIND OF OUTFIT DID SHE BUY WHEN SHE LOST WEIGHT?

Now arrange the circled letters to form the surprise answer, as suggested by the above cartoon.

Print answer here " ⃝⃝⃝⃝⃝⃝⃝⃝ "

JUMBLE®

Unscramble these four Jumbles, one letter to
each square, to form four ordinary words.

SOOGE

RAALT

HERETT

ENMECT

The charge is
burglary

My client
is plainly
innocent,
your honor

THE KIND OF CASE
HANDLED BY A
DEFENSE LAWYER.

Now arrange the circled letters to form the
surprise answer, as suggested by the above
cartoon.

Print answer here

JUMBLE®

Unscramble these four Jumbles, one letter to each square, to form four ordinary words.

LOGOI

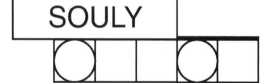

SOULY

YARPTS

NHEPAP

That's a lovely pattern

WHEN THEY LOOKED AT THE DISHES THROUGH THE STORE WINDOW, THEY SAW----

Now arrange the circled letters to form the surprise answer, as suggested by the above cartoon.

Print answer here "◯◯◯◯◯◯" ◯◯◯◯◯◯

Unscramble these four Jumbles, one letter to each square, to form four ordinary words.

SUMEO

PINYP

ULSSET

FORTYS

Your left, your left. I said your left, Jones

Boy, Sarge is mean

THE BEST WAY TO TEACH RECRUITS HOW TO MARCH.

Now arrange the circled letters to form the surprise answer, as suggested by the above cartoon.

Print answer here ⬡⬡⬡⬡ BY ⬡⬡⬡⬡

JUMBLE®

Unscramble these four Jumbles, one letter to
each square, to form four ordinary words.

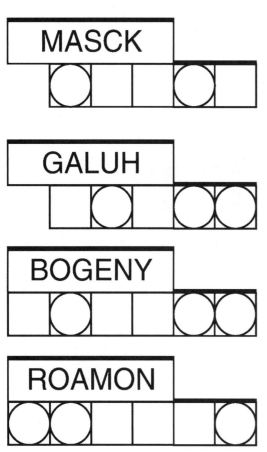

MASCK

GALUH

BOGENY

ROAMON

Look how quickly he's growing

I think he
just said
da da

EXPERIENCED BY
THE PARENTS OF A
FAST DEVELOP-
ING INFANT.

Now arrange the circled letters to form the
surprise answer, as suggested by the above
cartoon.

**Print
answer
here**

" "

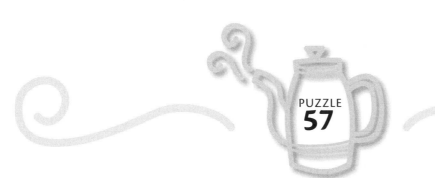

JUMBLE®

Unscramble these four Jumbles, one letter to each square, to form four ordinary words.

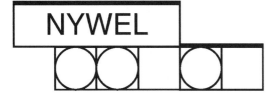

NYWEL

MOIFT

UNDIPT

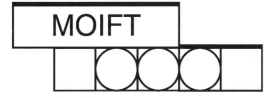

MARKEB

You'll be back in front of the cameras in no time

COUGH! COUGH!

THE DOCTOR TREATED THE COVER GIRL BECAUSE SHE WAS——

Now arrange the circled letters to form the surprise answer, as suggested by the above cartoon.

Print answer **A** *here*

" ◯◯◯◯◯ " ◯◯◯◯◯◯◯◯

JUMBLE®

Unscramble these four Jumbles, one letter to
each square, to form four ordinary words.

ARCTT

JOMAR

MUBHEL

ROBUGE

Hey, you guys,
get to work!

WHEN THE LUM-
BERJACKS FORMED
A JAZZ GROUP,
THEY ENDED UP
WITH A——

Now arrange the circled letters to form the
surprise answer, as suggested by the above
cartoon.

Print answer here ◯◯◯ " ◯◯◯ "

JUMBLE®

Unscramble these four Jumbles, one letter to each square, to form four ordinary words.

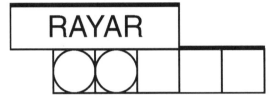

RAYAR

DAMAR

COBORN

BLUMFE

He relaxes by making the rounds

HOW THE MAE-STRO STUDIED THE SCORE FOR HIS NEXT CONCERT.

Now arrange the circled letters to form the surprise answer, as suggested by the above cartoon.

Print answer here

TO

JUMBLE.

Unscramble these four Jumbles, one letter to
each square, to form four ordinary words.

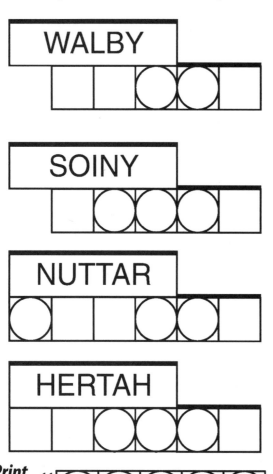

WALBY

SOINY

NUTTAR

HERTAH

I've waited a long
time for this

WHAT THE SEAM-
STRESS ENJOYED
ON HER WEDDING
DAY.

Now arrange the circled letters to form the
surprise answer, as suggested by the above
cartoon.

Print
answer
here " ⬡⬡⬡⬡⬡ - ⬡⬡⬡⬡⬡⬡ "

JUMBLE®

Unscramble these four Jumbles, one letter to each square, to form four ordinary words.

NUKKS

ROATA

FOLFAY

PANUCK

Good as new

Thanks, Doc. Back to the open sea

WHAT THE SAILOR EXPERIENCED WHEN HIS BROKEN LEG HEALED.

Now arrange the circled letters to form the surprise answer, as suggested by the above cartoon.

Print answer here **A** ⬡⬡⬡⬡ ⬡⬡⬡

JUMBLE®

Unscramble these four Jumbles, one letter to each square, to form four ordinary words.

YOIRN

MAGEL

LOPARR

ENBLIM

ALL-NIGHT DINER

Two coffees to go

WHEN CAN EVENING CLOTHES BE SEEN?

Now arrange the circled letters to form the surprise answer, as suggested by the above cartoon.

Print answer here

JUMBLE

Unscramble these four Jumbles, one letter to
each square, to form four ordinary words.

YAMEL

UVESA

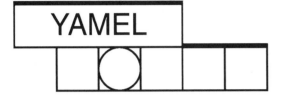

RENACK

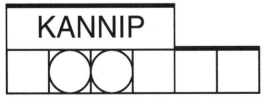

KANNIP

...and I say
to my esteemed
colleagues...

He's such
a blowhard

IN CONGRESS, YOU
CAN BE THIS EVEN
IF YOU'RE NOT----

Now arrange the circled letters to form the
surprise answer, as suggested by the above
cartoon.

Print answer here THE " ◯◯◯◯◯◯◯ "

JUMBLE®

Unscramble these four Jumbles, one letter to
each square, to form four ordinary words.

TENGA

PORRI

ORTETT

BILBEN

$5,000 to improve your smile

That's nothing
to laugh at

THE ESTIMATE FOR
BRACES LEFT HER
WITH---

Now arrange the circled letters to form the
surprise answer, as suggested by the above
cartoon.

*Print
answer
here*   A " "

Unscramble these four Jumbles, one letter to each square, to form four ordinary words.

HARAJ

KNOTE

WELLOY

LOTTEB

It's his first work in 10 — years

WHEN THE FAMED COMPOSER WROTE A NEW SCORE, IT WAS---

Now arrange the circled letters to form the surprise answer, as suggested by the above cartoon.

Print answer here " ◯◯◯◯◯◯◯◯◯◯◯ "

JUMBLE

Unscramble these four Jumbles, one letter to each square, to form four ordinary words.

LIFUD

FLEAY

THAILG

SULTYS

I was here first

No you weren't

I'll hold your coat

WHAT THE BOWL-ING DISPUTE TURNED INTO.

Now arrange the circled letters to form the surprise answer, as suggested by the above cartoon.

Print answer AN " ⬡⬡⬡⬡⬡ " ⬡⬡⬡⬡⬡ here

Unscramble these four Jumbles, one letter to each square, to form four ordinary words.

CUNEL

NEFTO

TRIOGE

ENCHIL

I'm studying subversive activities

I'm getting my masters

WHY THE SPIES WENT TO THE UNIVERSITY.

Now arrange the circled letters to form the surprise answer, as suggested by the above cartoon.

Print answer here FOR " ◯◯◯◯◯◯◯◯◯◯◯◯◯◯◯◯ "

JUMBLE

Unscramble these four Jumbles, one letter to each square, to form four ordinary words.

BITUC

SBAAH

BEWOLB

LARPIL

Dad, can I have 20 bucks?

AGAIN?!!

WHEN HIS SON ASKED FOR MONEY, DAD WAS LEFT IN A----

Now arrange the circled letters to form the surprise answer, as suggested by the above cartoon.

Print answer here "◯◯◯◯◯◯"

JUMBLE®

Unscramble these four Jumbles, one letter to each square, to form four ordinary words.

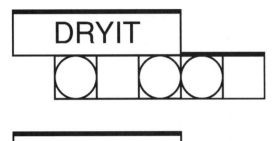

DRYIT

BASUQ

CLIFEK

RAJAUG

WHO WAS CALLED WHEN THE NEIGHBOR'S PARTY GOT TOO NOISY?

Now arrange the circled letters to form the surprise answer, as suggested by the above cartoon.

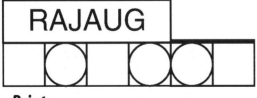

Print answer here THE " ⭘⭘⭘⭘⭘⭘ " ⭘⭘⭘⭘⭘

71

JUMBLE®

Unscramble these four Jumbles, one letter to
each square, to form four ordinary words.

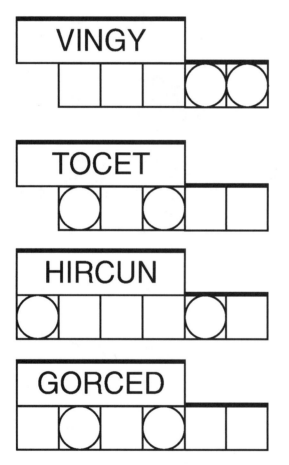

VINGY

TOCET

HIRCUN

GORCED

Say hello to the
nice man, Fifi

How can I
get away
from here?

WHAT THE INTRO-
VERT WANTED TO
BE WHEN HE WAS
STUCK AT THE
BORING PARTY.

Now arrange the circled letters to form the
surprise answer, as suggested by the above
cartoon.

Print answer here " ◯◯◯◯◯◯◯◯ "

JUMBLE®

Unscramble these four Jumbles, one letter to each square, to form four ordinary words.

SURUP

VELCO

SOOMER

STONEX

Where's the sun coming from?

HARD TO AVOID AT THE SEASHORE.

Now arrange the circled letters to form the surprise answer, as suggested by the above cartoon.

Print answer here " ☐☐☐☐☐☐☐☐☐☐☐☐☐ "

JUMBLE®

Unscramble these four Jumbles, one letter to each square, to form four ordinary words.

YOSUM

ZOONE

RICION

METIKS

I expect to be an officer

WHAT THE HOT-SHOT SALESMAN WANTED WHEN HE JOINED THE ARMY.

Now arrange the circled letters to form the surprise answer, as suggested by the above cartoon.

Print answer HIS " _____ "
here

JUMBLE®

Unscramble these four Jumbles, one letter to each square, to form four ordinary words.

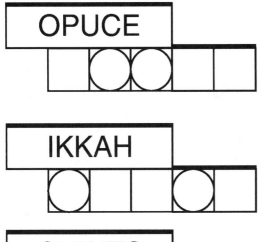

OPUCE

IKKAH

CHINTS

ASTOAN

He decked that bum in two rounds

She's gorgeous

FOR THE CHAMP, IT WAS A GOOD NIGHT FOR---

Now arrange the circled letters to form the surprise answer, as suggested by the above cartoon.

Print answer here " ◯◯◯◯◯◯◯◯◯◯ "

JUMBLE®

Unscramble these four Jumbles, one letter to each square, to form four ordinary words.

MORGO

LOUFT

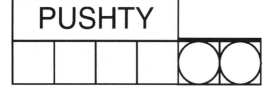

PUSHTY

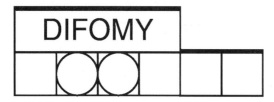

DIFOMY

Be careful, Helen, it could be fake

They're going like hotcakes

THE STREET PED- DLER'S WARES WERE ALWAYS---

Now arrange the circled letters to form the surprise answer, as suggested by the above cartoon.

Print answer here ⃝⃝⃝⃝ " ⃝⃝⃝ "

JUMBLE®

Unscramble these four Jumbles, one letter to each square, to form four ordinary words.

HARNC

RIGMY

PEXLUD

REMMIO

My, Harold, you do that so beautifully

THIS HELPS WHEN DOING THE DISHES.

Now arrange the circled letters to form the surprise answer, as suggested by the above cartoon.

Print answer here " ⭕⭕⭕ " ⭕⭕⭕⭕⭕⭕

JUMBLE®

Unscramble these four Jumbles, one letter to each square, to form four ordinary words.

MACHP

UGAVE

BISCER

CLUGED

I'm practicing my strokes

WHAT THE ART STUDENTS DID BEFORE THE BIG EXAM.

Now arrange the circled letters to form the surprise answer, as suggested by the above cartoon.

Print answer here " ◯◯◯◯◯◯◯◯ " ◯◯

JUMBLE

Unscramble these four Jumbles, one letter to
each square, to form four ordinary words.

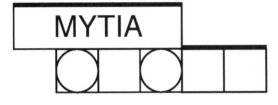

MYTIA

KERPI

LEHTAH

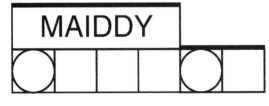

MAIDDY

Was the defendant
wearing this?

Yes

WHY THE SCARF
WAS INTRODUCED
AS EVIDENCE.

Now arrange the circled letters to form the
surprise answer, as suggested by the above
cartoon.

*Print answer
here* IT WAS "⟨⟩⟨⟩⟨⟩⟨⟩⟨⟩⟨⟩⟨⟩⟨⟩"

JUMBLE®

Unscramble these four Jumbles, one letter to each square, to form four ordinary words.

THANC

LYDOM

LOCASE

LEXFAN

No, George, that won't do

WHAT MUST BE LEARNED TO BECOME A DIA- MOND CUTTER?

Now arrange the circled letters to form the surprise answer, as suggested by the above cartoon.

Print answer here

" "

JUMBLE®

Unscramble these four Jumbles, one letter to each square, to form four ordinary words.

DEEXU

DARNB

NAKTIE

DIRNEH

I can't make enough loaves by myself

THE BAKER HIRED A HELPER BECAUSE HE HAD A----

Now arrange the circled letters to form the surprise answer, as suggested by the above cartoon.

Print answer here ⬡⬡⬡⬡⬡ ⬡⬡⬡⬡

JUMBLE®

Unscramble these four Jumbles, one letter to
each square, to form four ordinary words.

YASAS

VAGRE

GLEABE

WHOALL

Get out of my face

He's so cute
when he's mad

WHEN THE PAPA-
RAZZI ANGERED
THE TEEN IDOL,
HIS FANS FOUND
HIM---

Now arrange the circled letters to form the
surprise answer, as suggested by the above
cartoon.

Print answer here ◯◯◯ THE " ◯◯◯◯ "

JUMBLE®

Unscramble these four Jumbles, one letter to each square, to form four ordinary words.

REWAY

KULFE

DELIRB

NAWSER

Fruity with a bit of impudence

One of our best

WHERE THE CON-NOISSEUR WENT FOR A GOOD CABERNET.

Now arrange the circled letters to form the surprise answer, as suggested by the above cartoon.

Print answer here TO THE ⬜⬜⬜⬜ "⬜⬜⬜⬜⬜⬜⬜"

Unscramble these four Jumbles, one letter to each square, to form four ordinary words.

COPHE

LEVVA

DREEME

DYOMLE

I'm trying to bulk up

WHAT THE SCRAWNY WORKER DID IN THE DARK-ROOM.

Now arrange the circled letters to form the surprise answer, as suggested by the above cartoon.

Print answer here " ◯◯◯◯◯◯◯◯◯ "

JUMBLE®

Unscramble these four Jumbles, one letter to
each square, to form four ordinary words.

ACCOO

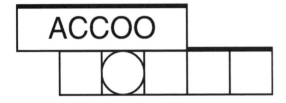

NALFK

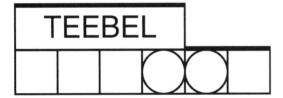

TEEBEL

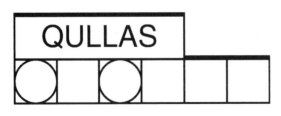

QULLAS

Your house could be
where the Ferris wheel is

Hi, Mommy

HOUSES
FOR
SALE

USING A CARNIVAL
TO DRAW CUS-
TOMERS TO HOME
SITES CREATED----

Now arrange the circled letters to form the
surprise answer, as suggested by the above
cartoon.

Print answer here "◯◯◯◯" OF ◯◯◯

JUMBLE®

Unscramble these four Jumbles, one letter to
each square, to form four ordinary words.

GOMEN

YAWNT

IMLYRG

ROBRAW

Dad, will you take
me to the mall?

After you
do the
grass

WHERE DAD
"DROVE" JUNIOR
WHEN HE ASKED
FOR A RIDE.

Now arrange the circled letters to form the
surprise answer, as suggested by the above
cartoon.

*Print
answer* TO THE
here

JUMBLE

Unscramble these four Jumbles, one letter to each square, to form four ordinary words.

ACNIP

LOVAC

CLURUN

DREHWS

Quick, turn around

Get out of the car with your hands up

Too late

SCREECH!

WHAT THE BANK ROBBERS FACED WHEN THEY HIT THE ROADBLOCK.

Now arrange the circled letters to form the surprise answer, as suggested by the above cartoon.

Print answer here A ⬡⬡⬡⬡⬡⬡⬡

JUMBLE®

Unscramble these four Jumbles, one letter to
each square, to form four ordinary words.

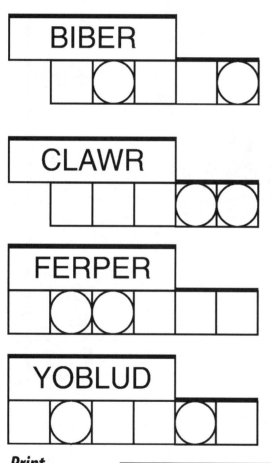

BIBER

CLAWR

FERPER

YOBLUD

It's
quitting
time

Let's finish—
I can use
the overtime

WHY THE CARPET
LAYERS WORKED
LATE.

Now arrange the circled letters to form the
surprise answer, as suggested by the above
cartoon.

*Print
answer
here* THEY ⬭⬭⬭⬭ ON A " ⬭⬭⬭⬭ "

JUMBLE®

Unscramble these four Jumbles, one letter to each square, to form four ordinary words.

COLIG

FORVA

BLOMAG

VINNET

Do you know what today is?

I haven't found anything worthy of my love for you

WHAT HUBBY GAVE HER WHEN HE FOR-GOT THEIR ANNIVERSARY.

Now arrange the circled letters to form the surprise answer, as suggested by the above cartoon.

Print answer here A "⬡⬡⬡⬡⬡" OF ⬡⬡⬡

JUMBLE®

Unscramble these four Jumbles, one letter to each square, to form four ordinary words.

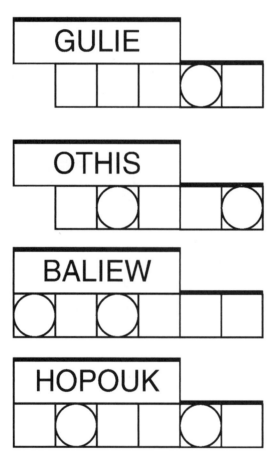

GULIE

OTHIS

BALIEW

HOPOUK

Want to go to a dance when you're done?

WHERE THE PARTY-GOERS INVITED THE MECHANIC.

Now arrange the circled letters to form the surprise answer, as suggested by the above cartoon.

Print answer here TO A " ◯◯◯◯◯◯◯ "

JUMBLE®

Unscramble these four Jumbles, one letter to
each square, to form four ordinary words.

RAWLD

LAFAT

GREATY

HEELAX

Hmm. Let's see.
Four clubs. No,
maybe three hearts

WHAT THE NOVICE'S
BRIDGE PARTNER
WANTED HER TO
BID---

Now arrange the circled letters to form the
surprise answer, as suggested by the above
cartoon.

Print answer here " ◯◯◯◯◯◯◯◯ "

JUMBLE®

Unscramble these four Jumbles, one letter to
each square, to form four ordinary words.

ASAIL

WOPOH

SUNDOL

AFAIRS

I don't know what to
say. I've looked everywhere

WHEN THE LIBRARIAN
MISPLACED THE
RARE DICTIONARY,
SHE WAS----

Now arrange the circled letters to form the
surprise answer, as suggested by the above
cartoon.

Print
answer AT A ⬡⬡⬡⬡ FOR " ⬡⬡⬡⬡⬡ "
here

JUMBLE

Unscramble these four Jumbles, one letter to each square, to form four ordinary words.

ONSOW

NALTS

BONDEY

NUMMAG

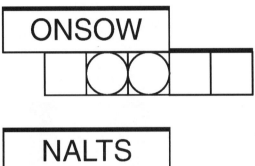

Bad dog. Look what you've done. Scoot!

WHAT MOM SAID WHEN THE PUPPY CHEWED ON THE TABLE LEG.

Now arrange the circled letters to form the surprise answer, as suggested by the above cartoon.

Print answer here "◯◯◯◯" ◯◯◯ ◯◯◯'◯

93

JUMBLE®

Unscramble these four Jumbles, one letter to
each square, to form four ordinary words.

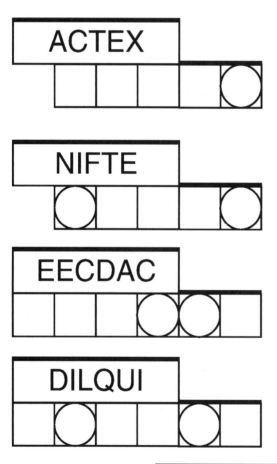

ACTEX

NIFTE

EECDAC

DILQUI

This makes
me look
like a
penguin

WHEN THE BRIDE-
GROOM GOT HIS
TUXEDO, HE WAS----

Now arrange the circled letters to form the
surprise answer, as suggested by the above
cartoon.

Print answer here ◯◯◯ TO BE " ◯◯◯◯ "

JUMBLE®

Unscramble these four Jumbles, one letter to each square, to form four ordinary words.

AMDAM

BEDIP

CARCIT

CLOPEM

Best wash I've had in a week

WHAT THE HOBO FELT LIKE WHEN HE GOT CAUGHT IN THE DOWNPOUR.

Now arrange the circled letters to form the surprise answer, as suggested by the above cartoon.

Print answer here A

95

JUMBLE®

Unscramble these four Jumbles, one letter to
each square, to form four ordinary words.

GYKAW

YILSK

COSTAM

TRIVEN

That dress makes
you look younger

This
old thing?

WHY HER HUSBAND
LIKED THE FORM-
FITTING OUTFIT.

Now arrange the circled letters to form the
surprise answer, as suggested by the above
cartoon.

**Print
answer
here** IT WAS ◯◯◯◯ ◯◯◯◯◯'◯

JUMBLE®

Unscramble these four Jumbles, one letter to each square, to form four ordinary words.

GLIBE

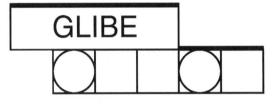

NORPE

PLINEP

LANARC

You'll be more comfortable without all those clothes

WELCOME

WHAT A GOOD SPORT WILL DO AT A NUDIST CAMP.

Now arrange the circled letters to form the surprise answer, as suggested by the above cartoon.

Print answer here

 AND  IT

JUMBLE®

Unscramble these four Jumbles, one letter to
each square, to form four ordinary words.

PRYAT

TILIM

CLAFIA

FEBRYL

That'll be $4,174

I'll take
care of
that

WHY SHE WENT
SHOPPING WITH
HER SUGAR DADDY.

Now arrange the circled letters to form the
surprise answer, as suggested by the above
cartoon.

Print answer here HE ◯◯◯ THE " ◯◯◯◯ "

JUMBLE®

Unscramble these four Jumbles, one letter to each square, to form four ordinary words.

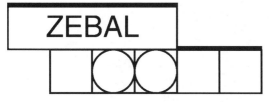

ZEBAL

CELRE

SLAVAS

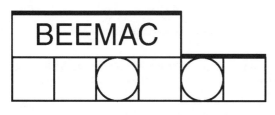

BEEMAC

This is a good way to meet people

Check your messages

WHAT THE POSTAL CLERK SOUGHT WHEN SHE WENT ONLINE FOR A DATE.

Now arrange the circled letters to form the surprise answer, as suggested by the above cartoon.

Print answer here "  "

JUMBLE®

Unscramble these four Jumbles, one letter to
each square, to form four ordinary words.

CUPAN

BEDAK

YEUFLE

YASMID

Gee, Marvin, this ball
has holes in it

WHEN THE "SMART"
GIRL WENT BOWL-
ING WITH HER DATE,
SHE---

Now arrange the circled letters to form the
surprise answer, as suggested by the above
cartoon.

*Print
answer
here*

⟨◯◯◯◯◯◯⟩ " ◯◯◯◯ "

JUMBLE®

Unscramble these four Jumbles, one letter to
each square, to form four ordinary words.

YANON

ANBLK

BORCAN

STRUME

We won!   I'm getting a new car   Let's go out on the town

WHAT THE FIREMEN
ENDED UP WITH
WHEN THEY WON
THE LOTTERY.

Now arrange the circled letters to form the
surprise answer, as suggested by the above
cartoon.

**Print answer
here** ◯◯◯◯◯ TO " ◯◯◯◯ "

101

JUMBLE®

Unscramble these four Jumbles, one letter to
each square, to form four ordinary words.

TALPI

WECIT

GEDDUR

BURNEM

We're number one!
We're number one!

WHEN THE MARCHING
BAND WON THE
SCHOOL COM-
PETITION, THEY----

Now arrange the circled letters to form the
surprise answer, as suggested by the above
cartoon.

**Print
answer
here** " ⭘⭘⭘⭘⭘⭘⭘⭘⭘⭘ " IT

Unscramble these four Jumbles, one letter to
each square, to form four ordinary words.

DAGUR

MUJOB

LENCAG

TIMOON

Ooops!   Not another
turnover

WHAT HAPPENED
TO THE BASKET-
BALL PLAYER WHO
COULDN'T
DRIBBLE?

Now arrange the circled letters to form the
surprise answer, as suggested by the above
cartoon.

Print
answer HE "   "
here

JUMBLE®

Unscramble these four Jumbles, one letter to each square, to form four ordinary words.

YIXTS

KANCK

TYLPEN

SEGOLP

It didn't work

Let's try again

WAS THE PRESCHOOLER ABLE TO TIE HIS SHOE ON THE FIRST TRY?

Now arrange the circled letters to form the surprise answer, as suggested by the above cartoon.

Print answer here " ◯◯◯◯ " ◯◯◯◯◯◯

Unscramble these four Jumbles, one letter to each square, to form four ordinary words.

YONPE

NAHVE

ZARWID

GAYMIB

He got 45 million

That'll give him something to chew on

SOLD

WHAT THE TYCOON RECEIVED WHEN HE SOLD THE GUM FACTORY.

Now arrange the circled letters to form the surprise answer, as suggested by the above cartoon.

Print answer here A "◯◯◯" OF ◯◯◯◯◯

JUMBLE®

Unscramble these four Jumbles, one letter to each square, to form four ordinary words.

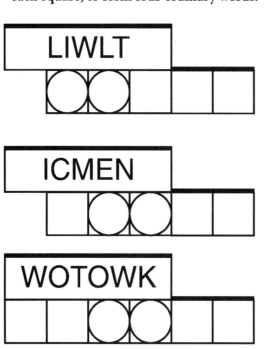

LIWLT

ICMEN

WOTOWK

YESGER

This new technique will increase productivity

HOW THE PRETZEL MAKER INCREASED BUSINESS.

Now arrange the circled letters to form the surprise answer, as suggested by the above cartoon.

Print answer here WITH A ◯◯◯ " ◯◯◯◯◯ "

JUMBLE®

Unscramble these four Jumbles, one letter to each square, to form four ordinary words.

GAADE

ELZAH

JADEGG

COLUSH

I knew it was going to happen

WHAT THE DOCTOR CONSIDERED THE MIND READER WHO FELL ON THE ICE.

Now arrange the circled letters to form the surprise answer, as suggested by the above cartoon.

Print answer here A " ⬭⬭⬭⬭ " ⬭⬭⬭⬭

JUMBLE®

Unscramble these four Jumbles, one letter to
each square, to form four ordinary words.

IMDEG

YINSH

ISWUNE

UNCLOM

I had so
much fun

The water
was refreshing

HOW THE FAMILY'S
DAY AT THE BEACH
TURNED OUT.

Now arrange the circled letters to form the
surprise answer, as suggested by the above
cartoon.

**Print answer
here**   "⬡⬡⬡⬡⬡⬡⬡⬡⬡⬡⬡⬡"

JUMBLE

Unscramble these four Jumbles, one letter to
each square, to form four ordinary words.

TABOL

BABIR

GROAND

BALLEF

These signs are making
me hungry and sleepy

BEST FOOD
TWO MILES

READING THE
ADVERTISING SIGNS
ON THE ROADSIDE
LEFT HIM---

Now arrange the circled letters to form the
surprise answer, as suggested by the above
cartoon.

*Print answer
here* ◯◯◯◯ " ◯◯◯◯◯ "

JUMBLE®

Unscramble these four Jumbles, one letter to each square, to form four ordinary words.

KIHCC

UFYSS

UNOFSI

PEBICS

...and then we got to the restaurant and then we met our friends and then...

Let's concentrate on our run. This slope is steep

WHAT SHE WANTED HER TALKATIVE SKI PARTNER TO DO.

Now arrange the circled letters to form the surprise answer, as suggested by the above cartoon.

Print answer here " ⬡⬡⬡⬡⬡⬡ "

110

JUMBLE®

Unscramble these four Jumbles, one letter to each square, to form four ordinary words.

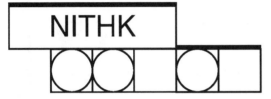

NITHK

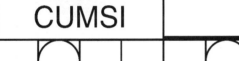

CUMSI

REPIME

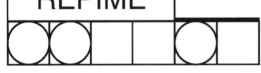

ROYSAR

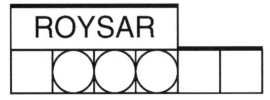

Poison ivy. Use this salve and stop slicing into the woods

WHAT THE SKIN DOCTOR GAVE THE GOLFER.

Now arrange the circled letters to form the surprise answer, as suggested by the above cartoon.

Print answer **A** "  "

JUMBLE®

Unscramble these four Jumbles, one letter to
each square, to form four ordinary words.

DAHEA

SNABI

LAPLOW

SHAWCE

Far
out!

Cool,
man

WHY THEY WATCHED
THE HULA DANCERS.

Now arrange the circled letters to form the
surprise answer, as suggested by the above
cartoon.

**Print
answer
here**

IT ◯◯◯ A " ◯◯◯ " ◯◯◯◯

JUMBLE®

Unscramble these four Jumbles, one letter to each square, to form four ordinary words.

ATLAN

SUROC

NAHZIG

INCLEY

I need help over here

WHAT THE MOVIE DIRECTOR ENDED UP WITH WHEN HE TRIED FLY-FISHING.

Now arrange the circled letters to form the surprise answer, as suggested by the above cartoon.

Print answer A here "◯◯◯◯◯◯◯◯" ◯◯◯◯◯

JUMBLE®

Unscramble these four Jumbles, one letter to
each square, to form four ordinary words.

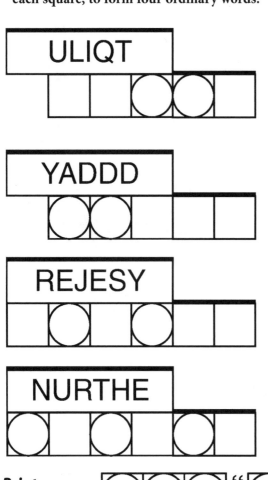

ULIQT

YADDD

REJESY

NURTHE

Beautiful
strokes

I'm giving
you an 'A'

HOW THE MANI-
CURE STUDENT
DID ON HER
FINAL EXAM.

Now arrange the circled letters to form the
surprise answer, as suggested by the above
cartoon.

**Print answer
here**

" " IT

JUMBLE®

Unscramble these four Jumbles, one letter to each square, to form four ordinary words.

YOAPS

INVEX

VEELEN

CHERAG

I put in the first load

Look at all those dials

WHAT MOM DID WHEN SHE GOT A NEW WASHING MACHINE.

Now arrange the circled letters to form the surprise answer, as suggested by the above cartoon.

Print answer here ⬡⬡⬡⬡ IT A "⬡⬡⬡⬡"

Unscramble these four Jumbles, one letter to each square, to form four ordinary words.

TONJI

YOANG

FAULED

DEECES

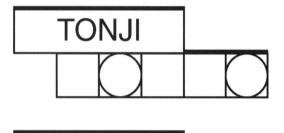

This one is only $25,000

EH?

WHEN THE SALES-MAN TOLD HIM WHAT THE DIAMOND COST, HE TURNED---

Now arrange the circled letters to form the surprise answer, as suggested by the above cartoon.

Print answer here   " ◯◯◯◯◯◯ " ◯◯◯◯

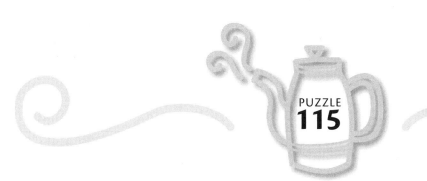

JUMBLE®

Unscramble these four Jumbles, one letter to each square, to form four ordinary words.

FRUOM

ANGLD

NAUMUT

PHISOL

Let's listen to our tape and improve our tones

WHAT THE BARBER-SHOP QUARTET USED TO PERFECT THEIR HARMONY.

Now arrange the circled letters to form the surprise answer, as suggested by the above cartoon.

Print answer here A " ⬚⬚⬚⬚⬚ " ⬚⬚⬚⬚

JUMBLE®

Unscramble these four Jumbles, one letter to
each square, to form four ordinary words.

LOFOD

RUZEA

FLIPER

UNCOOP

He's my
new
driver

Must be nice
to be related

THE CHIEF HIRED
HIS NEPHEW, WHO
AUTOMATICALLY
BECAME---

Now arrange the circled letters to form the
surprise answer, as suggested by the above
cartoon.

Print answer here " ⬤⬤⬤⬤ " - ⬤⬤⬤⬤⬤

JUMBLE®

Unscramble these four Jumbles, one letter to each square, to form four ordinary words.

NOJEY

MOVEN

GUEMLE

KAJECT

Three. The winning number is three

Boy, I needed that

WHAT HAPPENED WHEN THE ROULETTE PLAYER BET "ODD"?

Now arrange the circled letters to form the surprise answer, as suggested by the above cartoon.

Print answer here HE ◯◯◯ " ◯◯◯◯ "

JUMBLE®

Unscramble these four Jumbles, one letter to
each square, to form four ordinary words.

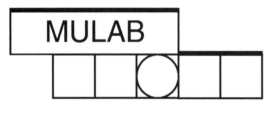

MULAB

BEESO

GIRLYS

PIMAGE

USUALLY FOUND
AT THANKSGIVING
DINNER.

Now arrange the circled letters to form the
surprise answer, as suggested by the above
cartoon.

Print answer here **A** " ◯◯◯◯◯◯◯◯◯ "

120

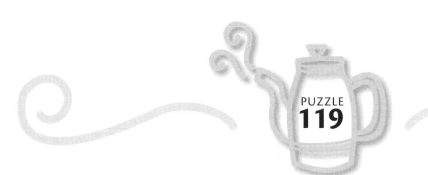

Unscramble these four Jumbles, one letter to each square, to form four ordinary words.

DRUGO

LURTY

DIELEY

ACTUFE

Am I doing this right? MOO!!

WHAT THE COW EXPERIENCED WHEN THE NOVICE TRIED TO MILK HER.

Now arrange the circled letters to form the surprise answer, as suggested by the above cartoon.

Print answer here " ◯◯◯◯◯◯ " ◯◯◯◯

121

JUMBLE®

Unscramble these four Jumbles, one letter to
each square, to form four ordinary words.

AIZME

FERIG

WARROH

TORFOG

It's a deal.
Congratulations
on your
new home

The
— check,
sir

HARD TO GET OUT
OF WITHOUT
PAYING.

Now arrange the circled letters to form the
surprise answer, as suggested by the above
cartoon.

Print answer here A ⃝⃝⃝⃝⃝⃝⃝⃝⃝⃝

Unscramble these four Jumbles, one letter to each square, to form four ordinary words.

KNARC

CANKS

SLAMEY

AERIPT

Oh, no! That's for the bake sale

I thought it was for me, your darling son

WHEN MOM HEARD JUNIOR'S EXCUSE, SHE SAID, "THAT---

Now arrange the circled letters to form the surprise answer, as suggested by the above cartoon.

Print answer here ⟪◯◯◯◯◯⟫ THE ⟪◯◯◯◯⟫"

JUMBLE®

Unscramble these four Jumbles, one letter to
each square, to form four ordinary words.

TAABE

ANBOT

BEHREY

FLEMSY

Your story doesn't add up

WHAT THE MATHE-
MATICIAN FACED
WHEN HE STAYED
OUT LATE.

Now arrange the circled letters to form the
surprise answer, as suggested by the above
cartoon.

*Print answer
here* THE ⬚⬚⬚⬚⬚ - ⬚⬚⬚⬚

JUMBLE®

Unscramble these four Jumbles, one letter to each square, to form four ordinary words.

CEKEH

RABIR

THIEFS

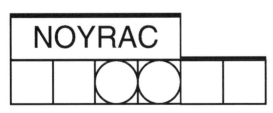

NOYRAC

Whew! I need a rest

WHEN THE FAMILY WENT ON VACATION, THEY TOOK---

Now arrange the circled letters to form the surprise answer, as suggested by the above cartoon.

Print answer here

125

JUMBLE®

Unscramble these four Jumbles, one letter to
each square, to form four ordinary words.

DABIE

VALGE

SIMPOE

YARPER

It's all mine. As far
as the eye can see

WHAT THE OILMAN
ENDED UP WITH
WHEN HE STRUCK
IT RICH.

Now arrange the circled letters to form the
surprise answer, as suggested by the above
cartoon.

**Print answer
here** A ⬜⭕⭕⭕ " ⭕⭕⭕⭕⭕⭕⭕ "

Unscramble these four Jumbles, one letter to each square, to form four ordinary words.

RAAMO

PYMUB

CEETIN

THROOC

Just a trim, sir?

WHAT THE BARBER STUDENT LEARNED WHEN HE CUT THE BALD MAN'S HAIR.

Now arrange the circled letters to form the surprise answer, as suggested by the above cartoon.

Print answer here

JUMBLE

Unscramble these four Jumbles, one letter to
each square, to form four ordinary words.

KOPER

FLONE

TYRRAM

APEARD

"The crook jumped over the fence."

...and the dot completes the thought."

2 years, 3 months, 4 days to go

THE PRISON CLASS LEARNED THAT THIS COMES AT THE END OF A SENTENCE.

Now arrange the circled letters to form the
surprise answer, as suggested by the above
cartoon.

Print answer here

JUMBLE®

Unscramble these four Jumbles, one letter to
each square, to form four ordinary words.

REVVE

POTIV

FLIEBE

JELOTS

Wake up, boys. Time
to go home

WHAT THE HOSTS
WERE STUCK WITH
WHEN THE PARTY
ENDED.

Now arrange the circled letters to form the
surprise answer, as suggested by the above
cartoon.

*Print answer
here* "〇〇〇〇〇〇〇〇〇"

129

JUMBLE®

Unscramble these four Jumbles, one letter to each square, to form four ordinary words.

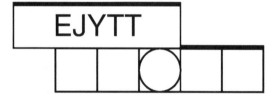

EJYTT

ZUFYZ

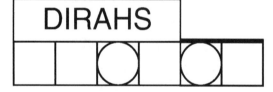

DIRAHS

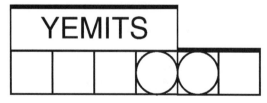

YEMITS

My fee is $100 a day plus extras

DEMANDED BY THE HOUSEKEEPER.

Now arrange the circled letters to form the surprise answer, as suggested by the above cartoon.

Print answer here A " ⃝⃝⃝⃝⃝ " ⃝⃝⃝

JUMBLE®

Unscramble these four Jumbles, one letter to
each square, to form four ordinary words.

FAHFC

WUNDE

ARTUNI

ARXOTH

48 easy payments of $700

Let's just
skip it

WHAT A SMART
BUYER WILL DO
WHEN THE PRICE IS
TOO HIGH.

Now arrange the circled letters to form the
surprise answer, as suggested by the above
cartoon.

Print answer here

131

JUMBLE®

Unscramble these four Jumbles, one letter to
each square, to form four ordinary words.

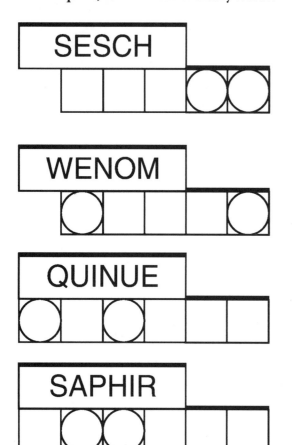

SESCH

WENOM

QUINUE

SAPHIR

This may be thousands
of years old. I'll
be famous

WHEN THE ARCHAE-
OLOGIST MADE AN
IMPORTANT FIND,
HIS CAREER----

Now arrange the circled letters to form the
surprise answer, as suggested by the above
cartoon.

*Print answer
here*

IN " "

JUMBLE®

Unscramble these four Jumbles, one letter to each square, to form four ordinary words.

MAFER

CIDDE

BRAJEB

BELUCK

Oh, no! Jackie told me it was casual

HOW SHE FELT WHEN SHE ARRIVED AT THE FANCY PARTY IN BLUE JEANS.

Now arrange the circled letters to form the surprise answer, as suggested by the above cartoon.

Print answer here " ◯◯◯ " ◯◯◯◯◯◯

JUMBLE®

Unscramble these four Jumbles, one letter to
each square, to form four ordinary words.

CUHLG

SUNEE

YORCUT

EEPPUK

I'll call you before your next appointment

WHAT A GOOD
MASSEUSE WILL
DO FOR HER
CUSTOMERS.

Now arrange the circled letters to form the
surprise answer, as suggested by the above
cartoon.

Print answer here ◯◯◯◯ IN "◯◯◯◯◯"

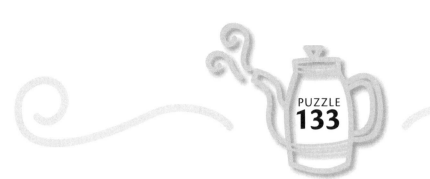

JUMBLE®

Unscramble these four Jumbles, one letter to each square, to form four ordinary words.

OSPOT

MOXIA

LOPPAR

BORREB

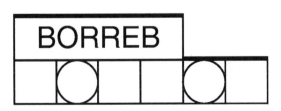

WHEN THE BARI-TONE TOOK A SHOWER, HE TURNED IT INTO A—

Now arrange the circled letters to form the surprise answer, as suggested by the above cartoon.

Print answer here " ⟨◯◯◯◯⟩ " ⟨◯◯◯◯◯◯⟩

JUMBLE®

Unscramble these four Jumbles, one letter to each square, to form four ordinary words.

AMMIX

PREYK

CUDINE

FLITUE

This is a nice place to relax after playing

WHAT THE BRITONS DID WHEN THEY FINISHED A ROUND OF GOLF.

Now arrange the circled letters to form the surprise answer, as suggested by the above cartoon.

Print answer here " ◯◯◯ - ◯◯ " IT ◯◯

JUMBLE®

Unscramble these four Jumbles, one letter to
each square, to form four ordinary words.

LUFET

SATTY

SLICHE

LADPIL

This is where the
admiral will board

THE SAILORS
SWABBED THE
PORT-SIDE DECK
BECAUSE IT WAS——

Now arrange the circled letters to form the
surprise answer, as suggested by the above
cartoon.

**Print
answer
here**

◯◯◯ ◯◯◯◯◯' ◯ " ◯◯◯◯ "

JUMBLE®

Unscramble these four Jumbles, one letter to
each square, to form four ordinary words.

MERIN

CUJIE

REPHEL

JINTEC

These shoes are sturdy and comfortable and improve your speed

That's a take

WHAT THE STAR
OUTFIELDER
TURNED INTO
WHEN HE GOT THE
ENDORSEMENT
DEAL.

Now arrange the circled letters to form the
surprise answer, as suggested by the above
cartoon.

Print answer here A " ◯◯◯◯◯◯◯ "

138

JUMBLE®

Unscramble these four Jumbles, one letter to each square, to form four ordinary words.

NOYOL

PRUCO

KEPCAT

YIKELL

Have you and Harold made up yet, Mildred?

MMPH....

HARD TO DO
WHEN VISITING
THE DENTIST.

Now arrange the circled letters to form the surprise answer, as suggested by the above cartoon.

Print answer here  " "

JUMBLE®

Unscramble these four Jumbles, one letter to each square, to form four ordinary words.

CRAFS

TOBOY

RIVUTE

KRUNEB

Nice going! You got them all again

WHAT THE HOME-RUN HITTER DID WHEN HE BOWLED THE LAST FRAME.

Now arrange the circled letters to form the surprise answer, as suggested by the above cartoon.

Print answer here " ◯◯◯◯◯◯◯ " ◯◯◯

JUMBLE®

Unscramble these four Jumbles, one letter to each square, to form four ordinary words.

HANNE

SELLI

RITHEH

HOTFUR

I want to leave everything to my nephew, the only one who visits me

He never goes out

WHAT THE RECLUSIVE MISER SOUGHT WHEN HE CHANGED HIS WILL.

Now arrange the circled letters to form the surprise answer, as suggested by the above cartoon.

Print answer here ◯◯◯◯◯◯ " ◯◯◯◯ "

JUMBLE®

Unscramble these four Jumbles, one letter to
each square, to form four ordinary words.

ENCIE

UPDYM

CHORCT

TORMIP

Looks like you're almost finished

THE SCULPTOR
WHISTLED WHILE
HE WORKED
BECAUSE HE
WAS——

Now arrange the circled letters to form the
surprise answer, as suggested by the above
cartoon.

**Print
answer IN A**
here " ⬡⬡⬡⬡⬡⬡⬡⬡ " ⬡⬡⬡⬡

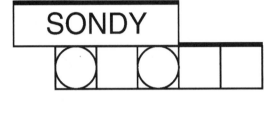

Unscramble these four Jumbles, one letter to each square, to form four ordinary words.

SONDY

GYROL

TEASET

MARPHE

Watch the light!

Slow down!

Don't get too close!

Relax

WHAT DAD TURNED INTO WHEN THE TEEN GOT HIS DRIVER'S LICENSE.

Now arrange the circled letters to form the surprise answer, as suggested by the above cartoon.

Print answer here A

JUMBLE®

Unscramble these four Jumbles, one letter to each square, to form four ordinary words.

TYTUP

SIPOE

LEPQUA

LIRIXE

You could paste wallpaper with this

Keep mixing and add water

WHAT THE COOK-ING STUDENT CRE-ATED WHEN SHE MADE GRAVY.

Now arrange the circled letters to form the surprise answer, as suggested by the above cartoon.

Print answer here ◯◯◯◯◯ A " ◯◯◯◯ "

144

JUMBLE®

Unscramble these four Jumbles, one letter to each square, to form four ordinary words.

PROAV

TAVIL

LAKLIA

IMCUPE

This can be dangerous.
Handle with care

HOW THE SCIEN-
TIST DESCRIBED
THE TOXIN-FILLED
TEST TUBE.

Now arrange the circled letters to form the surprise answer, as suggested by the above cartoon.

Print answer here A ⬜⬜⬜⬜⬜ ⬜⬜⬜⬜

JUMBLE®

Unscramble these four Jumbles, one letter to each square, to form four ordinary words.

WETHA

ORNOC

WURFOR

INGLEM

Now copy that 100 times

I will not talk in class

WHAT THE DISOBE-DIENT STUDENT HAD TO DO.

Now arrange the circled letters to form the surprise answer, as suggested by the above cartoon.

Print answer here " ⬡⬡⬡⬡⬡ " A ⬡⬡⬡⬡⬡⬡

JUMBLE®

Unscramble these four Jumbles, one letter to
each square, to form four ordinary words.

KULCC

CEKOH

LOYDOG

DAYPOR

It's so
pretty

So are
you

WHEN SHE SPOT-
TED THE RARE
SPECIES, THE BIRD-
WATCHERS SAID
SHE WAS----

Now arrange the circled letters to form the
surprise answer, as suggested by the above
cartoon.

**Print
answer
here** A ⬡⬡⬡⬡ " ⬡⬡⬡⬡⬡⬡ "

Unscramble these four Jumbles, one letter to
each square, to form four ordinary words.

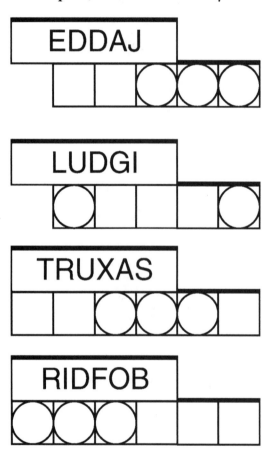

EDDAJ

LUDGI

TRUXAS

RIDFOB

Shut the window.
I've got the chills

WHAT THE SARGE
TURNED INTO
WHEN HE CAUGHT
A COLD.

Now arrange the circled letters to form the
surprise answer, as suggested by the above
cartoon.

*Print
answer
here*   A   " ⬡⬡⬡⬡⬡ "   ⬡⬡⬡⬡⬡⬡

JUMBLE®

Unscramble these four Jumbles, one letter to each square, to form four ordinary words.

CLICO

NOJAB

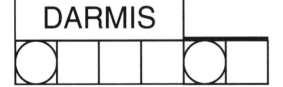

DARMIS

CAJALK

May I offer you a libation?

Thanks. Don't mind if I do

WHEN AN AFTER-DINNER DRINK WAS OFFERED, THE GUEST'S REPLY WAS———

Now arrange the circled letters to form the surprise answer, as suggested by the above cartoon.

Print answer here " ⭕⭕⭕⭕⭕⭕⭕ "

JUMBLE®

Unscramble these four Jumbles, one letter to
each square, to form four ordinary words.

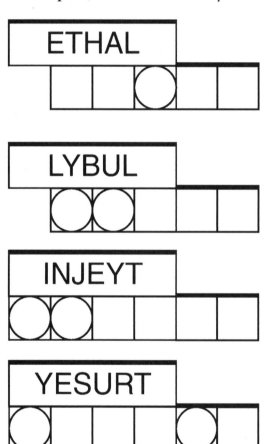

ETHAL

LYBUL

INJEYT

YESURT

Want some, Nellie?

WHAT HE GAVE THE
HORSE WHEN IT
OPENED ITS
MOUTH.

Now arrange the circled letters to form the
surprise answer, as suggested by the above
cartoon.

Print answer here

A " "

150

JUMBLE®

Unscramble these four Jumbles, one letter to each square, to form four ordinary words.

TAING

TAWLZ

LUFES

DOMBEY

My mortgage payment went up

You already make more than anybody

WHEN THE PILOT ASKED FOR A RAISE, HIS BOSS SAID----

Now arrange the circled letters to form the surprise answer, as suggested by the above cartoon.

Print answer here IT ◯◯◯◯◯◯ , ◯ " ◯◯◯ "

JUMBLE®

Unscramble these four Jumbles, one letter to each square, to form four ordinary words.

STUGE

ARRIF

MEEZYN

HEEBAD

Give me a call, gorgeous

Don't hold your breath

WHAT SHE HAD WHEN THE FLIRT-ING BAR-HOPPER GAVE HER HIS CARD.

Now arrange the circled letters to form the surprise answer, as suggested by the above cartoon.

Print answer here ◯◯◯ " ◯◯◯◯◯◯ "

JUMBLE®

Unscramble these four Jumbles, one letter to
each square, to form four ordinary words.

FROOG

POANI

URAUBE

ZENFRY

Hey, she's
choking me!

WHEN THE BLONDE
WRESTLED THE
BRUNETTE, SHE
FOUND HER——

Now arrange the circled letters to form the
surprise answer, as suggested by the above
cartoon.

Print answer here ⬡⬡ - " ⬡⬡⬡⬡⬡ "

Unscramble these four Jumbles, one letter to
each square, to form four ordinary words.

KASHY

EKQUA

HERTHS

VERHIT

I'll take
a jelly

Any glazed
left?

WHAT THE STAFF
TOOK BEFORE THE
MEETING STARTED.

Now arrange the circled letters to form the
surprise answer, as suggested by the above
cartoon.

*Print answer
here*

Unscramble these four Jumbles, one letter to each square, to form four ordinary words.

CUVOH

KLEAF

SIPCLE

UNBOYT

Whatta dump

Fold again

TOUGH TO DRAW AT A SEEDY POKER PARLOR.

Now arrange the circled letters to form the surprise answer, as suggested by the above cartoon.

Print answer here A " ⬡⬡⬡⬡ ⬡⬡⬡⬡⬡ "

JUMBLE®

Unscramble these four Jumbles, one letter to each square, to form four ordinary words.

ERECK

CADYE

SILFOS

RICCUS

Well, so much for a day of fishing

WHAT THE FASHION DESIGNER TURNED INTO WHEN THE STORM HIT.

Now arrange the circled letters to form the surprise answer, as suggested by the above cartoon.

Print answer here A "◯◯◯◯◯" ◯◯◯◯◯◯◯

156

JUMBLE®

Unscramble these four Jumbles, one letter to
each square, to form four ordinary words.

WROPE

DITAU

ETTORP

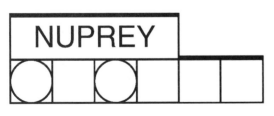

NUPREY

He's driving
me nuts

WHAT SHE WANTED
THE WHISTLING
PLUMBER TO DO.

Now arrange the circled letters to form the
surprise answer, as suggested by the above
cartoon.

Print answer here " ◯◯◯◯◯ " ◯◯◯◯◯

JUMBLE®

Unscramble these four Jumbles, one letter to each square, to form four ordinary words.

CANEP

NOAKE

SAMOUF

LOPPIN

You! Cut more vegetables. And you! Double the gravy! Step on it!

A CHEF MIGHT DO THIS ON A BUSY NIGHT.

Now arrange the circled letters to form the surprise answer, as suggested by the above cartoon.

Print answer here " ☐☐☐☐ " ☐☐ A ☐☐☐☐

JUMBLE®

Unscramble these four Jumbles, one letter to
each square, to form four ordinary words.

BOARR

HOPUC

MOYPLE

BREEMM

He doesn't seem to be tough now

WHEN THE GANG-
STER WAS JAILED,
HE WENT
FROM---

Now arrange the circled letters to form the
surprise answer, as suggested by the above
cartoon.

Print answer here ◯◯◯ TO ◯◯◯

JUMBLE®

Unscramble these four Jumbles, one letter to
each square, to form four ordinary words.

UNMOD

YENED

LURBIA

OIDING

The only thing I steer
these days is a tractor

WHAT THE PILOT
BECAME WHEN HE
BOUGHT A FARM.

Now arrange the circled letters to form the
surprise answer, as suggested by the above
cartoon.

Print answer here " "

160

JUMBLE®

Unscramble these four Jumbles, one letter to each square, to form four ordinary words.

NELLK

LEBLE

CRADOW

FLOAWL

The colors are breathtaking

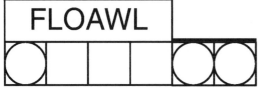

HOW THEY DESCRIBED THEIR AUTUMN WALK THROUGH THE WOODS.

Now arrange the circled letters to form the surprise answer, as suggested by the above cartoon.

Print answer here "◯◯◯◯◯◯ - ◯◯◯◯"

JUMBLE®

Unscramble these four Jumbles, one letter to each square, to form four ordinary words.

MATID

CREYD

RAYWEL

RODINO

Wash your clothes!

Mom, I'm shocked you said that

TO A SLOPPY TEENAGER, "LAUN- DRY" IS A---

Now arrange the circled letters to form the surprise answer, as suggested by the above cartoon.

Print answer here " ⬡⬡⬡⬡⬡ " ⬡⬡⬡⬡

Java
JUMBLE®

Challenger
Puzzles

JUMBLE®

Unscramble these six Jumbles, one letter to
each square, to form six ordinary words.

UFTOIT

FORREV

LICIAT

STEPEL

ROOVED

UNPOWT

Your body of
work has
improved

A PHOTOGRAPHER'S
JOB MAY DEPEND
ON THIS.

Now arrange the circled letters to form the
surprise answer, as suggested by the above
cartoon.

Print answer here

A "  "

JUMBLE®

Unscramble these six Jumbles, one letter to
each square, to form six ordinary words.

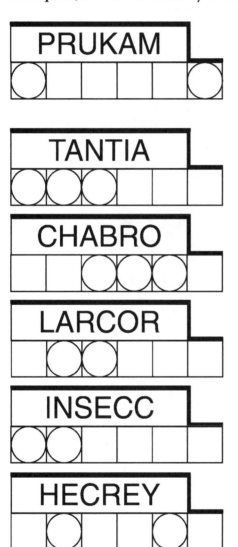

PRUKAM

TANTIA

CHABRO

LARCOR

INSECC

HECREY

We can get
that in here,
too

WHAT DAD TURNED
INTO ON GARBAGE
DAY.

Now arrange the circled letters to form the
surprise answer, as suggested by the above
cartoon.

Print answer here

A

165

JUMBLE®

Unscramble these six Jumbles, one letter to
each square, to form six ordinary words.

REESOI

SHUROC

NUBONI

ENCHEW

RANLYX

UNTRIP

Sell 5,000 at $47.50

AN EXECUTIVE
MIGHT DO THIS
DURING A BUSY
DAY.

Now arrange the circled letters to form the
surprise answer, as suggested by the above
cartoon.

Print answer here

166

JUMBLE®

Unscramble these six Jumbles, one letter to each square, to form six ordinary words.

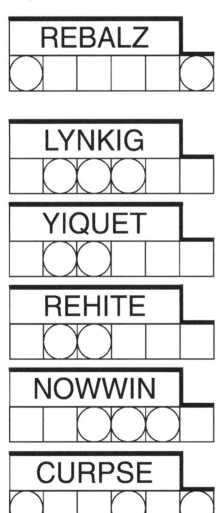

REBALZ

LYNKIG

YIQUET

REHITE

NOWWIN

CURPSE

Tell me again where you were last night

I need some sleep

FACED BY THE ARSON SUSPECT.

Now arrange the circled letters to form the surprise answer, as suggested by the above cartoon.

Print answer here

A

JUMBLE®

Unscramble these six Jumbles, one letter to
each square, to form six ordinary words.

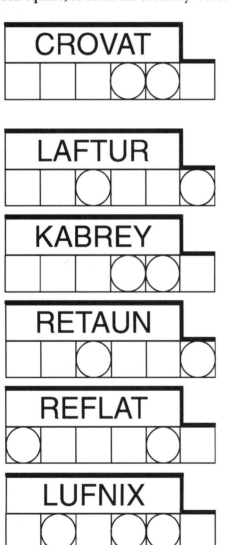

CROVAT

LAFTUR

KABREY

RETAUN

REFLAT

LUFNIX

I'm rich, but
I'm keeping
my job

Can you
give me
a loan?

WHEN SHE HIT THE
MILLION-DOLLAR
JACKPOT, THE
BANK CLERK
BECAME A----

Now arrange the circled letters to form the
surprise answer, as suggested by the above
cartoon.

Print answer here

" ◯◯◯◯◯◯◯ " ◯◯◯◯◯◯

JUMBLE®

Unscramble these six Jumbles, one letter to each square, to form six ordinary words.

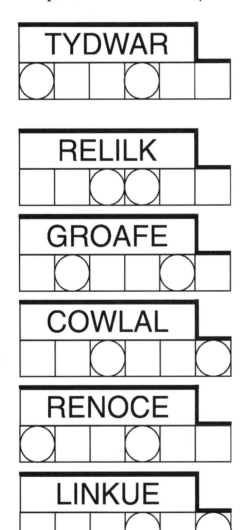

TYDWAR

RELILK

GROAFE

COWLAL

RENOCE

LINKUE

Oops—wrong valve

WHAT HAPPENED WHEN THE WILD-CATTER DRANK ON THE JOB?

Now arrange the circled letters to form the surprise answer, as suggested by the above cartoon.

Print answer here

HE ⭕⭕⭕ ⭕⭕⭕⭕⭕ " ⭕⭕⭕⭕⭕ "

JUMBLE®

Unscramble these six Jumbles, one letter to
each square, to form six ordinary words.

INDOAJ

ENVARG

CRAGOU

ENCOUB

RENUNG

GWEEDD

Don't worry. You'll do
fine 'til I get back

WHEN THE COWBOY
LEFT HIS HOME ON
THE RANGE, HE
GAVE HIS FAMILY
AN----

Now arrange the circled letters to form the
surprise answer, as suggested by the above
cartoon.

Print answer here

JUMBLE®

Unscramble these six Jumbles, one letter to
each square, to form six ordinary words.

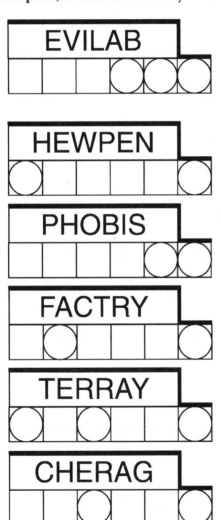

EVILAB

HEWPEN

PHOBIS

FACTRY

TERRAY

CHERAG

Au revoir. I'll be
back to get it
next month

WHAT SHE SAID
WHEN SHE BOUGHT
THE PARIS FASHION
ON LAYAWAY.

Now arrange the circled letters to form the
surprise answer, as suggested by the above
cartoon.

Print answer here

" ☐☐☐ " ☐☐☐ , ☐☐☐ ☐☐☐☐☐

PUZZLE
169

JUMBLE®

Unscramble these six Jumbles, one letter to each square, to form six ordinary words.

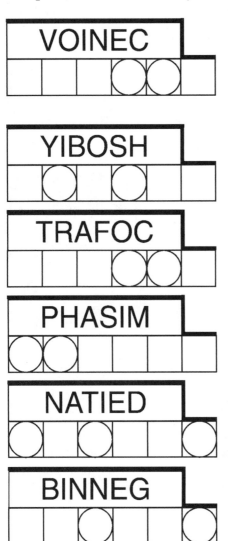

VOINEC

YIBOSH

TRAFOC

PHASIM

NATIED

BINNEG

Mommy, this tastes good

A CANDY CANE SHOULD BE CON-SUMED LIKE THIS.

Now arrange the circled letters to form the surprise answer, as suggested by the above cartoon.

Print answer here

IN " ⬡⬡⬡⬡ " ⬡⬡⬡⬡⬡⬡⬡⬡⬡⬡

JUMBLE®

Unscramble these six Jumbles, one letter to
each square, to form six ordinary words.

COABEN

SADLIM

PARTUB

SMURTI

GLAJEN

DANGIE

Does anybody
know what the
words mean?

WHAT THEY SANG
TO RING IN THE
NEW YEAR.

Now arrange the circled letters to form the
surprise answer, as suggested by the above
cartoon.

Print answer here

THE ⭕⭕⭕⭕⭕ " ⭕⭕⭕⭕ " ⭕⭕⭕⭕

JUMBLE®

Unscramble these six Jumbles, one letter to each square, to form six ordinary words.

PRETOY

MENUBB

QUORIL

YETLEE

DISMOW

NUDEAS

This sure is fun

That's my boy

WHEN JUNIOR HELPED DAD CUT THE GRASS, IT WAS——

Now arrange the circled letters to form the surprise answer, as suggested by the above cartoon.

Print answer here ◯◯◯◯◯◯ A " ◯◯◯-◯◯◯◯ "

JUMBLE®

Unscramble these six Jumbles, one letter to
each square, to form six ordinary words.

BLATOC

NICCIP

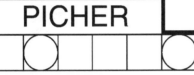

PICHER

CLIPAD

URGETT

NAANAB

We'll put
together
20,000 copies

Sign
here

THE BOOK PRINTER
OFFERED THE
AUTHOR----

Now arrange the circled letters to form the
surprise answer, as suggested by the above
cartoon.

Print answer here

A "⬡⬡⬡⬡⬡⬡⬡" ⬡⬡⬡⬡⬡⬡⬡⬡

JUMBLE®

Unscramble these six Jumbles, one letter to each square, to form six ordinary words.

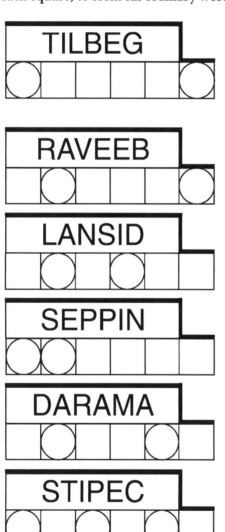

TILBEG

RAVEEB

LANSID

SEPPIN

DARAMA

STIPEC

Let's put it in second

GRR-SQUEAK   CLANK

WHAT THE EXOTIC DANCER DID WHEN SHE LEARNED TO DRIVE.

Now arrange the circled letters to form the surprise answer, as suggested by the above cartoon.

Print answer here

" ⟨◯◯◯◯◯◯◯◯◯⟩ " ⟨◯◯◯◯◯⟩

JUMBLE®

Unscramble these six Jumbles, one letter to
each square, to form six ordinary words.

SCYTIK

MNOMOC

NORBEK

BUSUDE

MOSHAN

TALLEB

Who's she
kidding?

49, 50, 51.
That's enough

HOW MANY CAN-
DLES WERE ON
THE AGING
BLONDE'S CAKE?

Now arrange the circled letters to form the
surprise answer, as suggested by the above
cartoon.

Print answer here

" ◯◯◯◯◯ ◯◯◯◯ " ◯◯◯◯

177

JUMBLE®

Unscramble these six Jumbles, one letter to
each square, to form six ordinary words.

DEDAHN

INGROI

CHUNAH

TYSSEM

HALDER

FRINIM

They're not flattering

WHY THE SHOPPER
DECIDED NOT TO
BUY THE TIGHT-
FITTING SLACKS.

Now arrange the circled letters to form the
surprise answer, as suggested by the above
cartoon.

Print answer here

SHE ◯◯◯◯ " ◯◯◯◯◯◯◯◯◯◯ "

JUMBLE®

Unscramble these six Jumbles, one letter to each square, to form six ordinary words.

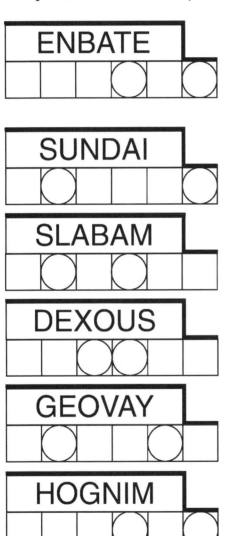

ENBATE

SUNDAI

SLABAM

DEXOUS

GEOVAY

HOGNIM

Way to go!

Thank you, young man

WHEN THE TEEN GAVE HIS SEAT TO THE LITTLE OLD LADY, HE ENDED UP IN----

Now arrange the circled letters to form the surprise answer, as suggested by the above cartoon.

Print answer here

JUMBLE®

Unscramble these six Jumbles, one letter to each square, to form six ordinary words.

THIRDE

UTTOWI

KLEREN

SMIHOD

TELTEK

HESKAN

Er...uh...lots of rain and windy unless the air currents shift. Then again...

WHAT THE FORE-CASTER DID WHEN HE WAS UNSURE OF HIS PREDIC-TION.

Now arrange the circled letters to form the surprise answer, as suggested by the above cartoon.

Print answer here

" ⃝⃝⃝⃝⃝⃝⃝⃝⃝ " THE ⃝⃝⃝⃝⃝

JUMBLE®

Unscramble these six Jumbles, one letter to each square, to form six ordinary words.

TUPSID

AIRWET

BUTSOE

RAHOTT

GATHUC

ONABBO

I left my wallet at the studio

WHEN THE MUSI-CIAN FORGOT HIS MONEY, HE WAS----

Now arrange the circled letters to form the surprise answer, as suggested by the above cartoon.

Print answer here

☐☐☐☐☐☐☐ " ☐☐☐☐☐ "

JUMBLE®

Unscramble these six Jumbles, one letter to
each square, to form six ordinary words.

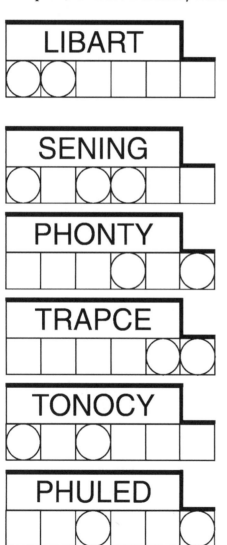

LIBART

SENING

PHONTY

TRAPCE

TONOCY

PHULED

Gloria
keeps her
figure

I've only got an hour
between meetings

WHEN THE EXECU-
TIVE ADDED YOGA
TO HER BUSY
SCHEDULE, SHE
WAS ---

Now arrange the circled letters to form the
surprise answer, as suggested by the above
cartoon.

Print answer here

" ⬭⬭⬭⬭⬭⬭⬭⬭⬭ " ⬭⬭⬭⬭

JUMBLE®

Unscramble these six Jumbles, one letter to
each square, to form six ordinary words.

SKABET

IMFLYS

KLARTE

ENOMAY

GANEET

BURGYB

Okay, boy. Nice
and easy

Charlie's got
a way
with him —

NEEDED TO CALM
A HIGH-STRUNG
RACEHORSE.

Now arrange the circled letters to form the
surprise answer, as suggested by the above
cartoon.

Print answer here

A " ◯◯◯◯◯◯ " ◯◯◯◯◯◯◯

Answers

1. **Jumbles:** CHASM HANDY MYRIAD FINITE
   Answer: When she got married, she went from—
   MAIDEN TO MAID

2. **Jumbles:** LAPEL HENCE ASTHMA DEPICT
   Answer: What the farmer did to stymie the chicken thief—
   "HATCHED" A PLAN

3. **Jumbles:** EXPEL SUITE BUTTON FERRET
   Answer: When he received the eviction notice, he—
   FELT "PUT OUT"

4. **Jumbles:** BASIC PURGE EROTIC WHALER
   Answer: What the feuding astronauts needed
   —THEIR "SPACE"

5. **Jumbles:** GOUGE BUSHY CAMPER PLOWED
   Answer: The shoemaker's sole companion—WAS A HEEL

6. **Jumbles:** CLOUT HABIT BALLAD JAILED
   Answer: What he ended up with when he finished his short
   story—A "TALL" TALE

7. **Jumbles:** RODEO OUNCE MORGUE BELONG
   Answer: The basketball player worked at the college bar
   because he was a—GOOD "BOUNCER"

8. **Jumbles:** FRANC ICILY FITFUL ZIGZAG
   Answer: What the detective was good at doing at a family
   gathering—"GRILLING"

9. **Jumbles:** LOVER TEASE PHYSIC UPWARD
   Answer: He quit his job at the sauna because it was a real—
   "SWEAT" SHOP

10. **Jumbles:** BIRCH BROIL POWDER MUFFLE
    Answer: What the math teacher considered the precocious
    pupil—A "PROBLEM" CHILD

11. **Jumbles:** CIVIL AGATE MYSTIC HUNGRY
    Answer: Girth can be turned into this—"RIGHT"

12. **Jumbles:** DIZZY VIRUS SAVAGE TAUGHT
    Answer: What she wore to the costume party—
    A GUY'S GUISE

13. **Jumbles:** SNORT TANGY DECODE MOHAIR
    Answer: When he won the poker tournament, he knew it
    was—IN THE CARDS

14. **Jumbles:** RUMMY THICK PALATE ADROIT
    Answer: What she got when she worked in her garden—
    THE "DIRT"

15. **Jumbles:** UPPER EXCEL FRACAS INVITE
    Answer: Easy for a general to command—RESPECT

16. **Jumbles:** LEAKY PROVE TEACUP INVEST
    Answer: When he took the astronomy class, he became a—
    "STAR" PUPIL

17. **Jumbles:** PIPER LANKY PSYCHE PATTER
    Answer: What it takes to write a song—PAPER AND PENCIL

18. **Jumbles:** YOUNG BERTH ACHING WORTHY
    Answer: When Junior said he didn't break the window, Dad
    saw—RIGHT THROUGH IT

19. **Jumbles:** FOAMY SWAMP EGOISM BECALM
    Answer: What the prison basketball team sadly lacked—
    "AWAY" GAMES

20. **Jumbles:** CRESS SYLPH POSTAL MAKEUP
    Answer: Important when shopping for eyeglasses—
    SPECS APPEAL

21. **Jumbles:** HAREM TONIC WISELY NINETY
    Answer: How the social climbers avoided being outsiders—
    THEY WENT IN

22. **Jumbles:** FLOUR NEWSY BOBBIN GENDER
    Answer: What he experienced when he lost the account—A
    "DOWNER"

23. **Jumbles:** LIBEL FLOOR MAYHEM FORMAT
    Answer: When the patrolman went undercover, he was—
    OFF "BEAT"

24. **Jumbles:** CLEFT BORAX LEVITY VIRILE
    Answer: Which of Einstein's theories can apply to
    marriage?—"RELATIVE-ITY"

25. **Jumbles:** FIFTY SKIMP HANGER SWIVEL
    Answer: Even a morning day-care worker can end up here—
    THE "SWING" SHIFT

26. **Jumbles:** MOOSE QUASH HECTIC VANDAL
    Answer: When the customers observed the watchmaker,
    they marveled at the—"HANDS" OF TIME

27. **Jumbles:** JOUST FUROR ENTITY FLAUNT
    Answer: What it took to repair the athlete's knee—
    A "JOINT" EFFORT

28. **Jumbles:** CHAFE LOUSE MORTAR NORMAL
    Answer: Why the maestro listened to the ball game—
    TO LEARN THE "SCORE"

29. **Jumbles:** RIGOR HUSKY MARROW GHETTO
    Answer: Preferred when traveling cross-country—
    THE "HIGH" WAY

30. **Jumbles:** CAKED LUCID NEARLY BABIED
    Answer: What the patrons did when the bar closed at
    midnight—CALLED IT A "DAY"

31. **Jumbles:** IVORY MONEY FIDDLE WALRUS
    Answer: Where he ended up when he got arrested—
    IN THE "UNDERWORLD"

32. **Jumbles:** LEAVE HAVOC ENDURE RADIAL
    Answer: When she took care of the injured puppy,
    he—"HEALED"

33. **Jumbles:** INKED SCOUT FORMAL CANOPY
    Answer: What she faced when he tried to cut in—
    ONE TOO MANY

34. **Jumbles:** CHIME EAGLE VERIFY DROPSY
    Answer: What the obstetrician and truck driver discussed—
    DELIVERIES

35. **Jumbles:** COMET FAUNA HOTBED LAUNCH
    Answer: When he bought the fabric store, he became a—
    MAN OF THE "CLOTH"

36. **Jumbles:** GRAIN PAUSE NOODLE CHERUB
    Answer: Sounded like this to his girlfriend—
    THE RUNAROUND

37. **Jumbles:** SHOWY LOOSE PRISON DARING
    Answer: Easy to avoid with a sunny disposition—
    A "SHADY" PERSON

38. **Jumbles:** LUSTY CURVE ABSORB FACADE
    Answer: What the golfing admiral did when it began
    raining—STAYED THE COURSE

39. **Jumbles:** CHAOS KNIFE ABDUCT TURGID
    Answer: Why the student dropped the history class—
    IT HAD NO "FUTURE"

40. **Jumbles:** UNIFY HOVEL CACTUS PAUNCH
    Answer: What his wife concluded he had when he went on
    an ice-cream diet—A "FAT" CHANCE

41. **Jumbles:** BUILT PATCH MUSKET DELUXE
    Answer: Why the orchestra functioned like clockwork—
    IT KEPT "TIME"

42. **Jumbles:** QUOTA ELEGY OPENLY ADJUST
    Answer: Often needed for a column—A PEDESTAL

43. **Jumbles:** DOUSE STOIC INNING FERVID
    Answer: In the military, additions can create—DIVISIONS

44. **Jumbles:** TYING FUDGE GIGOLO SMUDGE
    Answer: The fingerprint expert had a clean desk because he
    was—GOOD AT "DUSTING"

45. **Jumbles:** SOUSE GOING PURIFY LEAVEN
    Answer: What an "organ" can produce—A "GROAN"

46. **Jumbles:** WAGER GRIME INFANT GUITAR
    Answer: When the storm hit, the church bells in the small
    town were—"RINGING" WET

47. **Jumbles:** GROUP SWASH CALICO FLLUNKY
    Answer: What the aging beauty was able to keep when she
    had a face-lift—HER CHIN UP

48. **Jumbles:** COWER MURKY ECZEMA OXYGEN
    Answer: Why he worked at the mint—TO MAKE MONEY

49. **Jumbles:** KAPOK HUMID TUMULT STOOGE
Answer: Free cocktails on a flight can cause some passengers to be—UP, "TIGHT"

50. **Jumbles:** IDIOM KNEEL BLUISH FIZZLE
Answer: What the assistant did when the taxidermist took a vacation—"FILLED" IN

51. **Jumbles:** AWOKE DRYLY QUENCH LIZARD
Answer: The outlaws respected the artist because he was—QUICK ON THE "DRAW"

52. **Jumbles:** ADAPT BURLY CONVEX DREDGE
Answer: What kind of outfit did she buy when she lost weight?—"REDUCED"

53. **Jumbles:** GOOSE ALTAR TETHER CEMENT
Answer: The kind of case handled by a defense lawyer—ATTACHE

54. **Jumbles:** IGLOO LOUSY PASTRY HAPPEN
Answer: When they looked at the dishes through the store window, they saw—"PLATE" GLASS

55. **Jumbles:** MOUSE NIPPY TUSSLE FROSTY
Answer: The best way to teach recruits how to march—STEP BY STEP

56. **Jumbles:** SMACK LAUGH BYGONE MAROON
Answer: Experienced by the parents of a fast-developing infant—MANY "CHANGES"

57. **Jumbles:** NEWLY MOTIF PUNDIT EMBARK
Answer: The doctor treated the cover girl because she was—A "MODEL" PATIENT

58. **Jumbles:** TRACT MAJOR HUMBLE BROGUE
Answer: When the lumberjacks formed a jazz group, they ended up with a—LOG "JAM"

59. **Jumbles:** ARRAY DRAMA BRONCO FUMBLE
Answer: How the maestro studied the score for his next concert—FROM BAR TO BAR

60. **Jumbles:** BYLAW NOISY TRUANT HEARTH
Answer: What the seamstress enjoyed on her wedding day—"ALTAR-ATIONS"

61. **Jumbles:** SKUNK AORTA LAYOFF UNPACK
Answer: What the sailor experienced when his broken leg healed—A CAST OFF

62. **Jumbles:** IRONY GLEAM PARLOR NIMBLE
Answer: When can evening clothes be seen?—EARLY MORNING

63. **Jumbles:** MEALY SUAVE CANKER NAPKIN
Answer: In Congress, you can be this even if you're not—THE "SPEAKER"

64. **Jumbles:** AGENT PRIOR TOTTER NIBBLE
Answer: The estimate for braces left her with—TOO BIG A "BITE"

65. **Jumbles:** RAJAH TOKEN YELLOW BOTTLE
Answer: When the famed composer wrote a new score, it was—"NOTEWORTHY"

66. **Jumbles:** FLUID LEAFY ALIGHT STYLUS
Answer: What the bowling dispute turned into—AN "ALLEY" FIGHT

67. **Jumbles:** UNCLE OFTEN GOITER LICHEN
Answer: Why the spies went to the university—FOR "INTELLIGENCE"

68. **Jumbles:** CUBIT ABASH WOBBLE PILLAR
Answer: When his son asked for money, Dad was left in a—"LATHER"

69. **Jumbles:** DIRTY SQUAB FICKLE JAGUAR
Answer: Who was called when the neighbor's party got too noisy?—THE "RACKET" SQUAD

70. **Jumbles:** VYING OCTET URCHIN CODGER
Answer: What the introvert wanted to be when he was stuck at the boring party—"OUTGOING"

71. **Jumbles:** USURP CLOVE MOROSE SEXTON
Answer: Hard to avoid at the seashore—"OVEREXPOSURE"

72. **Jumbles:** MOUSY OZONE IRONIC KISMET
Answer: What the hotshot salesman wanted when he joined the army—HIS "COMMISSION"

73. **Jumbles:** COUPE KHAKI SNITCH SONATA
Answer: For the champ, it was a good night for—"KNOCKOUTS"

74. **Jumbles:** GROOM FLOUT TYPHUS MODIFY
Answer: The street peddler's wares were always—SOLD "OUT"

75. **Jumbles:** RANCH GRIMY DUPLEX MEMOIR
Answer: This helps when doing the dishes—"DRY" HUMOR

76. **Jumbles:** CHAMP VAGUE SCRIBE CUDGEL
Answer: What the art students did before the big exam—"BRUSHED" UP

77. **Jumbles:** AMITY PIKER HEALTH MIDDAY
Answer: Why the scarf was introduced as evidence—IT WAS "MATERIAL"

78. **Jumbles:** CHANT MOLDY SOLACE FLAXEN
Answer: What must be learned to become a diamond cutter?—MANY "FACETS"

79. **Jumbles:** EXUDE BRAND INTAKE HINDER
Answer: The baker hired a helper because he had a—KNEAD NEED

80. **Jumbles:** ASSAY GRAVE BEAGLE HALLOW
Answer: When the paparazzi angered the teen idol, his fans found him—ALL THE "RAGE"

81. **Jumbles:** WEARY FLUKE BRIDLE ANSWER
Answer: Where the connoisseur went for a good cabernet—TO THE WINE "SELLER"

82. **Jumbles:** EPOCH VALVE REDEEM MELODY
Answer: What the scrawny worker did in the darkroom—"DEVELOPED"

83. **Jumbles:** COCOA FLANK BEETLE SQUALL
Answer: Using a carnival to draw customers to home sites created—"LOTS" OF FUN

84. **Jumbles:** GNOME TAWNY GRIMLY BARROW
Answer: Where Dad "drove" Junior when he asked for a ride—TO THE LAWN MOWER

85. **Jumbles:** PANIC VOCAL UNCURL SHREWD
Answer: What the bank robbers faced when they hit the roadblock—A HOLDUP

86. **Jumbles:** BRIBE CRAWL PREFER DOUBLY
Answer: Why the carpet layers worked late—THEY WERE ON A "ROLL"

87. **Jumbles:** LOGIC FAVOR GAMBOL INVENT
Answer: What hubby gave her when he forgot their anniversary—A "GIFT" OF GAB

88. **Jumbles:** GUILE HOIST BEWAIL HOOKUP
Answer: Where the partygoers invited the mechanic—TO A "BLOWOUT"

89. **Jumbles:** DRAWL FATAL GYRATE EXHALE
Answer: What the novice's bridge partner wanted her to bid—"FAREWELL"

90. **Jumbles:** ALIAS WHOOP UNSOLD SAFARI
Answer: When the librarian misplaced the rare dictionary, she was—AT A LOSS FOR "WORDS"

91. **Jumbles:** SWOON SLANT BEYOND MAGNUM
Answer: What Mom said when the puppy chewed on the table leg—"GNAW" YOU DON'T

92. **Jumbles:** EXACT FEINT ACCEDE LIQUID
Answer: When the bridegroom got his tuxedo, he was—FIT TO BE "TIED"

93. **Jumbles:** MADAM BIPED ARCTIC COMPEL
Answer: What the hobo felt like when he got caught in the downpour—A DAMP TRAMP

94. **Jumbles:** GAWKY SILKY MASCOT INVERT
Answer: Why her husband liked the formfitting outfit—IT WAS LAST YEAR'S

95. **Jumbles:** BILGE PRONE NIPPLE CARNAL
Answer: What a good sport will do at a nudist camp—GRIN AND BARE IT

96. **Jumbles:** PARTY LIMIT FACIAL BELFRY
Answer: Why she went shopping with her sugar daddy—HE FIT THE "BILL"

97. Jumbles: BLAZE CREEL VASSAL BECAME
Answer: What the postal clerk sought when she went online for a date—"MALE" CALL

98. Jumbles: UNCAP BAKED EYEFUL DISMAY
Answer: When the "smart" girl went bowling with her date, she—PLAYED "DUMB"

99. Jumbles: ANNOY BLANK CARBON MUSTER
Answer: What the firemen ended up with when they won the lottery—MONEY TO "BURN"

100. Jumbles: PLAIT TWICE DRUDGE NUMBER
Answer: When the marching band won the school competition, they—"TRUMPETED" IT

101. Jumbles: GUARD JUMBO GLANCE MOTION
Answer: What happened to the basketball player who couldn't dribble?—HE GOT "BOUNCED"

102. Jumbles: SIXTY KNACK PLENTY GOSPEL
Answer: Was the preschooler able to tie his shoe on the first try?—"KNOT" LIKELY

103. Jumbles: PEONY HAVEN WIZARD BIGAMY
Answer: What the tycoon received when he sold the gum factory—A "WAD" OF MONEY

104. Jumbles: TWILL MINCE KOWTOW GEYSER
Answer: How the pretzel maker increased business—WITH A NEW "TWIST"

105. Jumbles: ADAGE HAZEL JAGGED SLOUCH
Answer: What the doctor considered the mind reader who fell on the ice—A "HEAD" CASE

106. Jumbles: MIDGE SHINY UNWISE COLUMN
Answer: How the family's day at the beach turned out—"SWIMMINGLY"

107. Jumbles: BLOAT RABBI DRAGON BEFALL
Answer: Reading the advertising signs on the roadside left him—BILL "BORED"

108. Jumbles: CHICK FUSSY FUSION BICEPS
Answer: What she wanted her talkative ski partner to do—"SCHUSS"

109. Jumbles: THINK MUSIC EMPIRE ROSARY
Answer: What the skin doctor gave the golfer—A "RASH" COMMENT

110. Jumbles: AHEAD BASIN WALLOP CASHEW
Answer: Why they watched the hula dancers—IT WAS A "HIP" SHOW

111. Jumbles: NATAL SCOUR HAZING NICELY
Answer: What the movie director ended up with when he tried fly-fishing—A "CASTING" CALL

112. Jumbles: QUILT DADDY JERSEY HUNTER
Answer: How the manicure student did on her final exam—SHE "NAILED" IT

113. Jumbles: SOAPY VIXEN ELEVEN CHARGE
Answer: What Mom did when she got a new washing machine—GAVE IT A "SPIN"

114. Jumbles: JOINT AGONY FEUDAL SECEDE
Answer: When the salesman told him what the diamond cost, he turned—"STONE" DEAF

115. Jumbles: FORUM GLAND AUTUMN POLISH
Answer: What the barbershop quartet used to perfect their harmony—A "SOUND" PLAN

116. Jumbles: FLOOD AZURE PILFER COUPON
Answer: The chief hired his nephew, who automatically became—"FIRE"-PROOF

117. Jumbles: ENJOY VENOM LEGUME JACKET
Answer: What happened when the roulette player bet "odd"?—HE GOT "EVEN"

118. Jumbles: ALBUM OBESE GRISLY MAGPIE
Answer: Usually found at Thanksgiving dinner—A "GOBBLER"

119. Jumbles: GOURD TRULY EYELID FAUCET
Answer: What the cow experienced when the novice tried to milk her—"UDDER" FEAR

120. Jumbles: MAIZE GRIEF HARROW FORGOT
Answer: Hard to get out of without paying—A MORTGAGE

121. Jumbles: CRANK SNACK MEASLY PIRATE
Answer: When Mom heard Junior's excuse, she said, "That—TAKES THE CAKE"

122. Jumbles: ABATE BATON HEREBY MYSELF
Answer: What the mathematician faced when he stayed out late—THE AFTER-MATH

123. Jumbles: CHEEK BRIAR FETISH CRAYON
Answer: When the family went on vacation, they took—IT EASY

124. Jumbles: ABIDE GAVEL IMPOSE PRAYER
Answer: What the oilman ended up with when he struck it rich—A BIG "SPREAD"

125. Jumbles: AROMA BUMPY ENTICE COHORT
Answer: What the barber student learned when he cut the bald man's hair—NOT MUCH

126. Jumbles: POKER FELON MARTYR PARADE
Answer: The prison class learned that this comes at the end of a sentence—FREEDOM

127. Jumbles: VERVE PIVOT BELIEF JOSTLE
Answer: What the hosts were stuck with when the party ended—"LEFTOVERS"

128. Jumbles: JETTY FUZZY RADISH STYMIE
Answer: Demanded by the housekeeper—A "TIDY" SUM

129. Jumbles: CHAFF UNWED NUTRIA THORAX
Answer: What a smart buyer will do when the price is too high—WITHOUT

130. Jumbles: CHESS WOMEN UNIQUE PARISH
Answer: When the archaeologist made an important find, his career—WAS IN "RUINS"

131. Jumbles: FRAME DICED JABBER BUCKLE
Answer: How she felt when she arrived at the fancy party in "blue" jeans—"RED" FACED

132. Jumbles: GULCH ENSUE OUTCRY UPKEEP
Answer: What a good masseuse will do for her customers—KEEP IN "TOUCH"

133. Jumbles: STOOP AXIOM POPULAR ROBBER
Answer: When the baritone took a shower, he turned it into a—"SOAP" OPERA

134. Jumbles: MAXIM PERKY INDUCE FUTILE
Answer: What the Britons did when they finished a round of golf—"TEA-ED" IT UP

135. Jumbles: FLUTE TASTY CHISEL PALLID
Answer: The sailors swabbed the port-side deck because it was—ALL THAT'S "LEFT"

136. Jumbles: MINER JUICE HELPER INJECT
Answer: What the star outfielder turned into when he got the endorsement deal—A "PITCHER"

137. Jumbles: LOONY CROUP PACKET LIKELY
Answer: Hard to do when visiting the dentist—TALK "OPENLY"

138. Jumbles: SCARF BOOTY VIRTUE BUNKER
Answer: What the home-run hitter did when he bowled the last frame—"STRUCK" OUT

139. Jumbles: HENNA LISLE HITHER FOURTH
Answer: What the reclusive miser sought when he changed his will—FRESH "HEIR"

140. Jumbles: NIECE DUMPY CROTCH IMPORT
Answer: The sculptor whistled while he worked because he was—IN A "CHIPPER" MOOD

141. Jumbles: SYNOD GLORY ESTATE HAMPER
Answer: What Dad turned into when the teen got his driver's license—A PASSENGER

142. Jumbles: PUTTY POISE PLAQUE ELIXIR
Answer: What the cooking student created when she made gravy—QUITE A "STIR"

143. Jumbles: VAPOR VITAL ALKALI PUMICE
Answer: How the scientist described the toxin-filled test tube—A VILE VIAL

144. Jumbles: WHEAT CROON FURROW MINGLE
Answer: What the disobedient student had to do—"WRITE" A WRONG

145. **Jumbles:** CLUCK CHOKE GOODLY PARODY
Answer: When she spotted the rare species, the bird-watchers said she was—A GOOD "LOOKER"

146. **Jumbles:** JADED GUILD SURTAX FORBID
Answer: What the sarge turned into when he caught a cold—A "DRAFT" DODGER

147. **Jumbles:** COLIC BANJO DISARM JACKAL
Answer: When an after-dinner drink was offered, the guest's reply was—"CORDIAL"

148. **Jumbles:** LATHE BULLY JITNEY SURETY
Answer: What he gave the horse when it opened its mouth—JUST A "BIT"

149. **Jumbles:** GIANT WALTZ USEFUL EMBODY
Answer: When the pilot asked for a raise, his boss said—IT WOULDN'T "FLY"

150. **Jumbles:** GUEST FRIAR ENZYME BEHEAD
Answer: What she had when the flirting bar hopper gave her his card—HIS "NUMBER"

151. **Jumbles:** FORGO PIANO BUREAU FRENZY
Answer: When the blonde wrestled the brunette, she found her—UN-"FAIR"

152. **Jumbles:** SHAKY QUAKE THRESH THRIVE
Answer: What the staff took before the meeting started—THEIR SEATS

153. **Jumbles:** VOUCH FLAKE SPLICE BOUNTY
Answer: Tough to draw at a seedy poker parlor—A "FULL HOUSE"

154. **Jumbles:** CREEK DECAY FOSSIL CIRCUS
Answer: What the fashion designer turned into when the storm hit—A "SLICK" DRESSER

155. **Jumbles:** POWER AUDIT POTTER PENURY
Answer: What she wanted the whistling plumber to do—"PIPE" DOWN

156. **Jumbles:** PECAN OAKEN FAMOUS POPLIN
Answer: A chef might do this on a busy night—"COOK" UP A PLAN

157. **Jumbles:** ARBOR POUCH EMPLOY MEMBER
Answer: When the gangster was jailed, he went from—MOB TO MOP

158. **Jumbles:** MOUND NEEDY BURIAL INDIGO
Answer: What the pilot became when he bought a farm—"GROUNDED"

159. **Jumbles:** KNELL BELLE COWARD FALLOW
Answer: How they described their autumn walk through the woods—"WONDER-FALL"

160. **Jumbles:** ADMIT DECRY LAWYER INDOOR
Answer: To a sloppy teenager, "laundry" is a—"DIRTY" WORD

161. **Jumbles:** OUTFIT FERVOR ITALIC PESTLE OVERDO UPTOWN
Answer: A photographer's job may depend on this—A "POSITIVE" REVIEW

162. **Jumbles:** MARKUP ATTAIN BROACH CORRAL SCENIC CHEERY
Answer: What Dad turned into on garbage day—A TRASH COMPACTOR

163. **Jumbles:** SOIREE CHORUS BUNION WHENCE LARYNX TURNIP
Answer: An executive might do this during a busy day—EXERCISE OPTIONS

164. **Jumbles:** BLAZER KINGLY EQUITY EITHER WINNOW SPRUCE
Answer: Faced by the arson suspect—A BURNING QUESTION

165. **Jumbles:** CAVORT ARTFUL BAKERY NATURE FALTER INFLUX
Answer: When she hit the million-dollar jackpot, the bank clerk became a—"FORTUNE" TELLER

166. **Jumbles:** TAWDRY KILLER FORAGE CALLOW ENCORE UNLIKE
Answer: What happened when the wildcatter drank on the job?—HE GOT WELL "OILED"

167. **Jumbles:** ADJOIN GRAVEN COUGAR BOUNCE GUNNER WEDGED
Answer: When the cowboy left his home on the range, he gave his family an—ENCOURAGING WORD

168. **Jumbles:** VIABLE NEPHEW BISHOP CRAFTY ARTERY CHARGE
Answer: What she said when she bought the Paris fashion on layaway—"BYE" NOW, PAY LATER

169. **Jumbles:** NOVICE BOYISH FACTOR MISHAP DETAIN BENIGN
Answer: A candy cane should be consumed like this—IN "MINT" CONDITION

170. **Jumbles:** BEACON DISMAL ABRUPT TRUISM JANGLE GAINED
Answer: What they sang to ring in the New Year—THE SAME "AULD" SONG

171. **Jumbles:** POETRY BENUMB LIQUOR EYELET WISDOM SUNDAE
Answer: When Junior helped Dad cut the grass, it was—QUITE A "MOW-MENT"

172. **Jumbles:** COBALT PICNIC CIPHER PLACID GUTTER BANANA
Answer: The book printer offered the author—A "BINDING" CONTRACT

173. **Jumbles:** GIBLET BEAVER ISLAND PEPSIN ARMADA SEPTIC
Answer: What the exotic dancer did when she learned to drive—"STRIPPED" GEARS

174. **Jumbles:** STICKY COMMON BROKEN SUBDUE HANSOM BALLET
Answer: How many candles were on the aging blonde's cake?—"COUNT LESS" ONES

175. **Jumbles:** HANDED ORIGIN HAUNCH SYSTEM HERALD INFIRM
Answer: Why the shopper decided not to buy the tight-fitting slacks—SHE HAD "HINDSIGHT"

176. **Jumbles:** BEATEN UNSAID BALSAM EXODUS VOYAGE HOMING
Answer: When the teen gave his seat to the little old lady, he ended up in—GOOD "STANDING"

177. **Jumbles:** DITHER OUTWIT KERNEL MODISH KETTLE SHAKEN
Answer: What the forecaster did when he was unsure of his prediction—"WHETHERED" THE STORM

178. **Jumbles:** STUPID WAITER OBTUSE THROAT CAUGHT BABOON
Answer: When the musician forgot his money, he was—WITHOUT "NOTES"

179. **Jumbles:** TRIBAL ENSIGN PYTHON CARPET TYCOON UPHELD
Answer: When the executive added yoga to her busy schedule, she was—"STRETCHED" THIN

180. **Jumbles:** BASKET FLIMSY TALKER YEOMAN NEGATE GRUBBY
Answer: Needed to calm a high-strung racehorse—A "STABLE" TRAINER

Need More Jumbles®?

Jumble® Books

More than 175 puzzles each!

Jammin' Jumble®
$9.95 • ISBN: 1-57243-844-4

Java Jumble®
$9.95 • ISBN: 978-1-60078-415-6

Jazzy Jumble®
$9.95 • ISBN: 978-1-57243-962-7

Jet Set Jumble®
$9.95 • ISBN: 978-1-60078-353-1

Joyful Jumble®
$9.95 • ISBN: 978-1-60078-079-0

Juke Joint Jumble®
$9.95 • ISBN: 978-1-60078-295-4

Jumble® at Work
$9.95 • ISBN: 1-57243-147-4

Jumble® Celebration
$9.95 • ISBN: 978-1-60078-134-6

Jumble® Explosion
$9.95 • ISBN: 978-1-60078-078-3

Jumble® Fever
$9.95 • ISBN: 1-57243-593-3

Jumble® Fiesta
$9.95 • ISBN: 1-57243-626-3

Jumble® Fun
$9.95 • ISBN: 1-57243-379-5

Jumble® Madness
$9.95 • ISBN: 1-892049-24-4

Jumble® Mania
$9.95 • ISBN: 1-57243-697-2

Jumble® See & Search
$9.95 • ISBN: 1-57243-549-6

Jumble® See & Search 2
$9.95 • ISBN: 1-57243-734-0

Jumble® Surprise
$9.95 • ISBN: 1-57243-320-5

Jumpin' Jumble®
$9.95 • ISBN: 978-1-60078-027-1

Outer Space Jumble®
$9.95 • ISBN: 978-1-60078-416-3

Rainy Day Jumble®
$9.95 • ISBN: 978-1-60078-352-4

Ready, Set, Jumble®
$9.95 • ISBN: 978-1-60078-133-0

Sports Jumble®
$9.95 • ISBN: 1-57243-113-X

Summer Fun Jumble®
$9.95 • ISBN: 1-57243-114-8

Travel Jumble®
$9.95 • ISBN: 1-57243-198-9

TV Jumble®
$9.95 • ISBN: 1-57243-461-9

Jumble® Genius
$9.95 • ISBN: 1-57243-896-7

Jumble® Grab Bag
$9.95 • ISBN: 1-57243-273-X

Jumble® Jackpot
$9.95 • ISBN: 1-57243-897-5

Jumble® Jambalaya
$9.95 • ISBN: 978-1-60078-294-7

Jumble® Jamboree
$9.95 • ISBN: 1-57243-696-4

Jumble® Jubilee
$9.95 • ISBN: 1-57243-231-4

Jumble® Juggernaut
$9.95 • ISBN: 978-1-60078-026-4

Jumble® Junction
$9.95 • ISBN: 1-57243-380-9

Jumble® Jungle
$9.95 • ISBN: 978-1-57243-961-0

Oversize Jumble® Books

More than 500 puzzles each!

Generous Jumble®
$19.95 • ISBN: 1-57243-385-X

Giant Jumble®
$19.95 • ISBN: 1-57243-349-3

Gigantic Jumble®
$19.95 • ISBN: 1-57243-426-0

Jumbo Jumble®
$19.95 • ISBN: 1-57243-314-0

The Very Best of Jumble® BrainBusters
$19.95 • ISBN: 1-57243-845-2

Jumble® Crosswords™

More than 175 puzzles each!

More Jumble® Crosswords™
$9.95 • ISBN: 1-57243-386-8

Jumble® Crosswords™ Jackpot
$9.95 • ISBN: 1-57243-615-8

Jumble® Crosswords™ Jamboree
$9.95 • ISBN: 1-57243-787-1

Jumble® BrainBusters™

More than 175 puzzles each!

Jumble® BrainBusters™
$9.95 • ISBN: 1-892049-28-7

Jumble® BrainBusters™ II
$9.95 • ISBN: 1-57243-424-4

Jumble® BrainBusters™ III
$9.95 • ISBN: 1-57243-463-5

Jumble® BrainBusters™ IV
$9.95 • ISBN: 1-57243-489-9

Jumble® BrainBusters™ 5
$9.95 • ISBN: 1-57243-548-8

Jumble® BrainBusters™ Bonanza
$9.95 • ISBN: 1-57243-616-6

Boggle™ BrainBusters™
$9.95 • ISBN: 1-57243-592-5

Boggle™ BrainBusters™ 2
$9.95 • ISBN: 1-57243-788-X

Jumble® BrainBusters™ Junior
$9.95 • ISBN: 1-892049-29-5

Jumble® BrainBusters™ Junior II
$9.95 • ISBN: 1-57243-425-2

Fun in the Sun with Jumble® BrainBusters™
$9.95 • ISBN: 1-57243-733-2